WINDS
of
CHANGE

WINDS
of
CHANGE

The Future of Democracy in Iran

REZA PAHLAVI

Since 1947
**REGNERY
PUBLISHING, INC.**
An Eagle Publishing Company • Washington, DC

Copyright © 2002 by Reza Pahlavi

Library of Congress Cataloging-in-Publication Data

Pahlavi, Reza, 1960–
    Winds of change : the future of democracy in Iran / Reza Pahlavi.
      p. cm.
    ISBN 0-89526-191-X
      1. Democracy—Iran. 2. Iran—Politics and government—1979– I. Title.

JQ1789.A15 P35 2001
320.955—dc21
2001048440

Published in the United States by
Regnery Publishing, Inc.
An Eagle Publishing Company
One Massachusetts Avenue, NW
Washington, DC 20001
www.regnery.com

Distributed to the trade by
National Book Network
4720-A Boston Way
Lanham, MD 20706

Printed on acid-free paper
Manufactured in the United States of America

10 9 8 7 6 5 4 3 2 1

BOOK DESIGN BY JULIE LAPPEN
SET IN GARAMOND 3

Books are available in quantity for promotional or premium use. Write to Director of Special Sales, Regnery Publishing, Inc., One Massachusetts Avenue, NW, Washington, DC 20001, for information on discounts and terms or call (202) 216-0600.

To the memory of
all our fallen heroes and patriots

To learn more about Reza Pahlavi and the campaign
to bring secularism and democracy to Iran,
visit www.rezapahlavi.org

CONTENTS

INTRODUCTION

his book is dedicated to the future of Iran and to my compatriots, especially today's young generation. Each one of us wants the best for our country, even when our views differ on how to achieve it. But at this point in our history, our situation is tragic. Our country is mired in backwardness, obscurantism, rigidity, radicalism, poverty, corruption, and incivility—all at the hands of a clerical dictatorship. Yet our countrymen everywhere yearn to move Iran back into the modern age and to build a future that reflects our historic aspirations achieved through the natural gifts of our people.

I strongly believe that, as much as possible, people need to be aware of all the visions and ideas available, before they can make a responsible choice. For this reason I have written this book: to inform my compatriots as well as all other interested persons of my vision of Iran's future.

In one sense, I have a special connection to Iran's past through the circumstances of my birth. But in another sense, I am just another Iranian, deeply disturbed by the present and seriously concerned about the future of my country. I write as a passionate citizen with a deep sense of duty. Along with many of my dedicated and committed compatriots, I look at our national predicament and strive to find solutions.

It may come as a great surprise to millions of Iranians that I am often thought to hold certain notions that have no part in my thinking process. It is precisely for this reason that I have put my principles and ideas in writing so that my compatriots, no matter where they may be, can not only evaluate for themselves what I actually think, but also prepare themselves for the challenges that lie ahead as we strive to carry out our patriotic and civic duties.

I am often asked about my views regarding the era preceding the clerical regime. Clearly, there are legitimate reasons for criticizing various issues and factors that contributed to the political crisis resulting in clerical rule. In retrospect, however, most Iranians will agree with me that Iran would have taken a different path, which would have brought us different results, had it had a chance to weather the storm and fine-tune its course, rather than abandon altogether what existed.

Each one of us has ideas about how our past national leaders could have best advanced our country. As a heterogeneous society, gifted with a rich and complex cultural and political history, Iranians have a multitude of views about past controversies. It will serve little constructive purpose to rehash old arguments. This book is about our future, our goals, our passionate desire to find solutions, our collective need to move forward in the interest of today's youth, and for the sake of our future generations.

Today, Iranians remain greatly worried about the state of their homeland. We suffer insurmountable economic problems under the present regime; we are ruled by a theocracy that is out of touch with our people's real aspirations while the future of our nation is a daily concern.

It is easy to talk about determining our own future, but, of course, much harder to achieve it. As noted, Iran has a politically diverse society, with a broad spectrum of outlooks, philosophies, and ideologies. There are leftists and rightists, monarchists and republicans, conservatives, centrists, and liberals—all of whom love their country, but who envision its future development from different perspectives.

As a diverse society, one of our main challenges is to demonstrate our ability to agree on a common agenda for the salvation of our homeland. My objective is to rally the people of Iran under one basic principle without advocating any particular ideology or form of government, in the sense of preempting a due political process. It advocates what I believe to be a common denominator for the good of all: self-determination.

My goal is to encourage Iranians to set aside their differences, to eschew their personal ideals and political ideologies. I ask them to consider adopting this basic agenda:

- To promote a national consensus on key issues such as the need for democracy, secularism, human rights, and popular sovereignty;
- To adopt a robust yet nonviolent political strategy for bringing about political change;
- To set the stage for an all-inclusive national referendum, with international observation, enabling the people of Iran to determine the type of democratic government they wish for their homeland.

It is neither my role nor my responsibility to predetermine what specific social, economic and political program is best for Iran in the coming decades. Instead, I do feel an obligation to set forth my own views on the present crisis, how we can change the situation, and how we can work together to build a new society and political order that reflect the will of the people. I do not represent any particular group in Iran, but the interests of all. I hope to reach as many people as possible across a wide spectrum. I want to talk about issues that concern all of us, both within the country and among the large Iranian community abroad, many of whom are looking forward to the day they will finally be able to return home, roll up their sleeves, and contribute to the development of their country.

As a member of a generation that has been a victim of circumstances, I too share the pain. Like others in my generation, I have been deeply affected by the events of the last few decades. But unlike others, I carry the heavy burden of public expectations that come with my name.

Sadly, I was forced to live in exile. But because of it, I have benefited from the opportunity to live among individuals from all walks of life. My unrestricted encounters and in-depth conversations with people, some of them with no knowledge of who I was, have exposed me to the reality of their lives, thus enlightening and preparing me in ways unimaginable before my exile. Not many with my background have had the opportunity to develop their views, unfiltered, by having also had the experience of living as a regular citizen—the opportunity to travel around the world and experience different cultures, values, and political environments, like everyone else.

In the last twenty-one years, many Iranians have had varied opinions and expectations about the nature of my role in leading our national struggle for freedom. While some have sought to define my role exclusively through the prism of a 2,500-year-old institution—the monarchy—I see myself, beyond the implications of my last name, as an Iranian burdened with the responsibility to look to the future, not the past. Today, our national commitment must be to unify our voices, put an end to repression, and bring solid democratic footing to our homeland. Whether as a nation we then opt for a constitutional monarchy or a republic will be exclusively determined by the people of Iran by means of a democratic process: a national referendum.

Clearly, Iranians will have little tolerance for individual absolute rule—be it that of a monarch, a president, or a supreme clerical leader. A democratic

Iran will guarantee a system of government, popularly based, and with clear delineation of power with "checks and balances." This will ensure a vibrant civil society wherein people of different ethnicities, religions, socioeconomic groups, and political persuasions will coexist peacefully while rebuilding their homeland.

For the world community, Iran remains a complex problem. For over two decades, it has experienced an Iran mired with chaos, violence, the seizure of hostages, angry mobs, senseless slogans, war, murder, and assassinations—in short, a total disregard for fundamental human values and civility.

Yet, at the time of this writing, the American government, other major world powers, and particularly the Western media have persisted in inaccurately portraying the political dynamics in Iran as a struggle between a "reformist" Mr. Khatami and "radical conservatives." Understandably, the world community is puzzled about how to react to Iran: which statement, which slogan, which faction, and which promise to believe?

The real struggle taking shape in Iran today is not between Khatami and other clerics; rather, it is the forces of state despotism and terrorism against an emerging popular movement that demands democracy, rejects militant fundamentalism, and repudiates "supreme rule," allegedly by "divine right."

Today's generation of young Iranians who grew up after the 1979 upheaval will soon make up three-quarters of the population. The relevant questions that ought to be asked about Iran are: What is the composition of this emerging generation? What are its aspirations? Where does it want to go from here?

It is incumbent upon the older generation to be in touch with the younger generation and to keep these questions always in the forefront. Failure to notice and close any gap that may exist between their outlook and that of today's youth would seriously challenge our national opportunity to bring about change to our political predicament. The ability to address the demands of our citizens must be the only litmus test for any government that aims to bring progress to our homeland.

Where do we go from here? Iran can ill afford yet another bloody upheaval. Instead, we must look for ways to implement and accelerate an evolutionary process out of our current impasse. My passion and personal commitment is to bring about political change in Iran by way of civil disobedience and non-violent action.

Most Iranians today are deeply discouraged by the state of our nation. Ever since the clerics took over, the very word "Iranian" has taken on a negative connotation in the minds of many around the world, which unfairly associates it with savagery, injustice, and fanaticism. This negative image has deeply troubled many in our state of exile. At times, we have conveniently referenced ourselves as "Persians," in an attempt to disassociate ourselves from the angry, hostile, and virulent face of the clerical regime in Tehran. Today, the once respected citizen of Iran endures the humiliating experience of being fingerprinted at international borders, as if they were all criminals.

One of my goals for Iran is to continue what my grandfather started—the restoration of pride in the words "Iran" and "Iranian." As Iranians, we need not be ashamed of our political past. A century ago, our country was ranked among the undeveloped and backward nations. The Constitutional Revolution of 1906 brought us a democratic parliamentary system in place of an absolute monarchy. Later, my grandfather was instrumental in preserving our territorial integrity and in setting Iran on the path to modernity. During his short tenure, he managed to lead and transform Iran from a poor, disease-ridden, and chaotic country into a secure, progressive nation.

At an early age, my father took responsibility of an Iran occupied by foreign forces. Under his leadership, the country rid itself of the occupiers and, in a relatively short time, transformed Iran into a unified, prospering nation. Ironically, some have argued that the crisis of the late seventies was due, in part, to an excessively rapid rate of growth and modernization. During the same period, unfortunately the democratic process was curtailed and did not keep pace. This contributed greatly to the political crisis that preceded the 1979 upheaval. Flying in the face of a previously modernizing Iran, the clerical regime ushered in extremism and militancy, thereby antagonizing the world and miring our country in costly isolation.

Iran's destiny will ultimately be determined by its own citizens. Iranians are a gifted people with a great civilization, yet they value modernity as they do their ancient traditions. But time is running out, and the process must start now.

This book focuses on several key areas. First, I have presented my personal philosophy and attitudes as I evaluate our past, our present, and the future. Second, I have set forth my thoughts on the direction my compatriots may wish to consider as we plan and look toward a dynamic future. Finally, I have offered solutions about how to break out of the present impasse. Winds of change are sweeping through Iran. The clerical regime is bracing itself for an irreversible downward phase. Important days and events lie ahead. We must handle the forthcoming transition wisely and prudently if we are to avoid another plunge into yet another dictatorship. How can we plan for this? How can we ensure a smooth transition to democracy?

What can we do as individuals and as a community to bring about positive change?

The answer lies in a collective, united front, working together in finding solutions to our problems. Let us therefore join hands and commit all our efforts towards making such a future a reality.

CHAPTER 1

MY VISION AND OUTLOOK

hile my name is known to all Iranians, I regret that my views are less well known, especially to Iranians in our homeland. Because I believe that it is critical that my thought process and core beliefs be well understood by as many Iranians as possible, I would like to offer here some basic principles that underlie my thinking about the future of our country.

In a free, open, and democratic system, it is quite natural that, if the people agree with, and embrace, the views of a particular movement or leader, that movement or leader may ultimately be provided the opportunity to implement those views. With this premise,

my ability to offer the symbolic leadership Iran needs
lies in the acceptance of my views by my compatriots.

The past twenty-two years have given me plenty
of opportunities to develop and refine my thinking
about the predicament of our country. My views have
resulted from my exposure to a multitude of opinions of friends as well as foes; I did not limit myself
to talking just to my supporters. One of the earliest
lessons life taught me was the critical importance of
seeking the truth. In the political scene, the full pic-
ture, and hence the truth, can only come from knowing alternative points of view. The strength of a good
leader comes from being exposed to diverse ideologies and opinions; decisions cannot be based solely
on the counsel of advisory groups, all cut from the
same cloth.

Ever since childhood, I have despised hollow flat-
tery and blindly obedient yes-men. Today, my closest
advisors are aware that I demand truthful and factual
opinions. Of course, our traditional culture is filled
with elaborate courtesies and complex relationships.
But the false advice and selective reporting my father

received from some people was ultimately a betrayal, not only of him, but, more importantly, of the people. With this as a constant reminder, I regularly solicit the viewpoint of as many people with different ideologies as possible.

On the international scene, I benefited from interaction with world leaders, including monarchs, presidents, prime ministers and party leaders, political and scholastic figures, and prominent members of the business community. I studied their experiences and methodologies, and exchanged ideas and suggestions. This provided me with a great deal of insight into the feasibility of a variety of social, economic and political models, which in turn led me to conclude that, despite our unique circumstances, our problems do have solutions. In fact, governments around the globe face a multitude of similar problems, and address them by utilizing solutions derived from a variety of models and methods. All this is done in an atmosphere of freedom and open debate, and through the interaction of governments with NGOs and academics, both domestically and internationally. If the Iranian problem-solving model is to be successful, our country must have a similar atmosphere of openness.

This experience has been a great crucible in which to hammer out my own political thinking and philosophy over the years. I am optimistic because I believe there are indeed ways out of our present predicament. The cynicism and despair that afflict many of our countrymen is the main symptom of our closed and repressive environment. They have no opportunity to engage in open and public debate, analyze the nature of a variety of problems, or question the legitimacy of the clerical regime as a whole.

In this context, I wish to present the principles and values that form my vision in respect to Iran:

First, I believe that self-determination is the essential centerpiece and key to nearly all our aspirations. The absence of democracy has been one of our greatest sources of weakness and vulnerability in the past. What Iran lacks is not so much the concept of democracy as the practical experience of working to implement it. We are paying the price today.

Thus, attaining freedom for Iran is my number one goal. Without it we have no foundation. That I am the son of the last Shah of Iran is well known, but it is not the issue. My only goal is to establish a secular democracy in Iran. Our countrymen have to be liberated first. I am well aware that, at this point, any discussion of a monarchy in Iran—or a republic for that matter—would be divisive. And it would compromise the vital issue of unity at this critical period in our history. The merits of the institution that I represent can be weighed only after we actually have a political order based on self-determination and genuine democracy. At this moment, Iranians must not be distracted from placing the democratic process at the top of the list of national priorities.

But why have we had problems in the past with establishing a democratic leadership? The reasons are many, but I think we need to start with the national psyche of our country—a tendency to look up to a sword-bearing man on horseback, or some kind of "savior" in whom all faith can be placed. As a student of our own history, I affirm that Iranians no

longer need to wait for the arrival of a "savior," that
in fact, we, the people, are riding that horse, and our
will is our sword.

Iran has gone through tragic and dark times over
the past two decades, affecting every single one of us,
wherever we may be. But I trust we have learned
something from this experience. We cannot look to
some great leader to come in and give us solutions on
a platter, to bestow upon us a good life, ready-made.
We must start from scratch. Striving to make Iran a
great country is a patriotic duty and task for all of us.
We therefore have to make certain that we commit
our best efforts towards its realization. Responsibility
for choices, and their consequences, must rest with
the people. Thus I insist that democratization, above
all else, is the prerequisite for our success. The exact
form of democracy can be decided later through
national debate and referendum.

Second, we must look to the future and not to
the past. Many events have occurred over the past
half century, filling us all with diverse emotions.
Whatever we may think about the past, what was

good and what was not, we need to remember that even the best of yesterday cannot address the needs of today. Each era has its particular set of circumstances and requirements. We need to understand them fully as we strive to build our future. We have no time, nor should we have the desire, for vengeance. We all have grievances about various things, but these that can mire us in the endless, ugly process of settling old scores. Our country needs to get on with the new agenda.

Third, we have to renew and strengthen our traditions and the practice of tolerance. Our country is a rich mosaic of different religious, ethnic, and political groups. No one group can be allowed to dominate, and everyone must feel at home in our shared motherland. We have to recognize that the views and aspirations among the population will differ to some extent, and that we must accommodate these differences. It is time we reestablish our roots of social, religious, and ethnic tolerance. This does not only mean that we allow for the presence of those who think differently, but that we recognize diversity itself as the bedrock of democracy—that it guarantees a lively civil society.

Fourth, communication—a central tool affecting virtually every aspect of our times—is the critical link to success. With this in mind, I believe in open dialog and communication with the disillusioned within the current regime. Dialog and open communication will not only serve as an important tool to facilitate and enhance the pace of change, but more importantly, it will avoid pushing the hardliners into a corner, whereby they could stifle the small breathing space our courageous youth have been fighting for in their struggle to gain complete freedom. In this respect, dialog does not suggest that the shortcomings of the clerical regime are justified or that the system should be legitimized.

Fifth, we require a healing process. It has taken a whole generation for people to be able to view the prerevolutionary era in a clear perspective. It will take even longer before we fully understand the implications of a generation coming of age under clerical rule. Already we are witnessing a change of heart by many of the same people who actively helped bring about the clerical regime. But even more than their parents, the children of the revolution who consider themselves innocent victims are well justified in claiming their right to determine their own future, and not remain stuck with the results brought about by the older generation. Fortunately, emotions are being set aside, and people are looking at the whole process more objectively. In every corner of our country, Iranians openly question the clerical regime, and seek solutions that would get our country back on track. If the original intent was to seek more freedom, clearly we have witnessed its opposite. The goal remains the same, but innocence has been replaced by a political awareness. The past national frenzy was based far more on emotions than on rational thinking. Reconciliation is now essential.

Sixth, the principles of peaceful evolution, nonviolence, and reconciliation on the political level are at the heart of my thinking. If Iran is to start operating as a genuine democracy, Iranians will need to put aside their prejudices, phobias, paranoia, and bitterness, and demonstrate their ability to maintain unity in diversity.

Some Iranians tell me I am naive or excessively idealistic when I term nonviolence a basic principle. But I embrace nonviolence as a tested, practical approach to change. Mahatma Gandhi and Dr. Martin Luther King, just to name two, succeeded through nonviolence against great odds. But I also recognize that nonviolence cannot work unless the regime in question is entering a crisis stage, filled with self-doubt, as I believe many ruling Iranian clerics are doing. Signs show that pragmatic elements within this regime may be thinking about a way out of the present impasse.

But how do we handle this process? The good news is that the situation in Tehran, in broad terms, seems to be heading in the right direction. The regime is losing confidence in itself. Even those high up are aware of widespread dissatisfaction and anger on the part of the population and do not want to push for a replay of 1979. Many in the regime also realize that mass coercion against the people is no longer a good option.

While espousing nonviolence, however, we cannot be naive. I do not believe for a minute that people should passively accept brutality and repression. Indeed, should the regime sense imminent collapse, and decide to hold onto power by raw force and terror, the people have a legitimate right to defend themselves. Nor would the world community allow such genocidal activity. I hope the situation will not come to that, and that the regime will recognize the inevitable and act accordingly. For the desired scenario is not a bloody revolution, but a peaceful evolution—the only process that will bring about lasting change without uprooting all social foundations.

In tactical terms, the clerics must be allowed a workable exit. A peaceful transition will get the clerics out of the halls of government and back to their respected positions in the mosques—not in a humiliating way, but in recognition of their own interests and that of Islam.

Since the religious factor has been one of the most important issues consuming our society in recent decades, I would like to elaborate further on the subject of religion and the role of the clergy in our society. Many Westerners, unaware of Iranian history, have developed the impression that Islam has always been central to our governing process, and that Iranians' religious beliefs have barred them from espousing the principles of separation of church (in this case, the Shiite clerical structure) and state. Nothing can be further from the truth. In reality, Iran has experimented for several centuries with various degrees and models of governance, quite independent of religion.

However, a profound personal commitment to faith has been deeply rooted in Iranian culture and heritage. As one of the cradles of civilization, Iran has been a land of tolerance, a home to a multitude of ethnicities and religions. The respect for individual faith gained root and flourished in our land, and our forefathers were among the first to introduce the concept of a deity and of monotheism to mankind. In all these years, men of the cloth, regardless of which faith they represented, were respected members of our society.

Since the advent of Islam, our clergymen have served as a moral compass. Spirituality has been an inseparable part of our culture. And our men of the cloth have been respected by the various sectors of our society.

But the advent of an Islamic theocracy in 1979 introduced a totally different role of religion and clergy. For the first time, these revolutionary clerics stepped out of the mosques and entered the political arena. Rather than being moral advisers to society, they became the decision makers and attempted to manage the daily affairs of the country. Even worse, they attempted to rewrite our history, our culture, and our traditions.

Soon, the once revered clergy had to provide daily answers to the most difficult social, economic, and policy questions. When their answers fell short, so did reverence to them.

Today, moral guidance has been replaced by clerical censorship and dictatorial fiat. Daily, the ruling clerics in Tehran pass judgments on which newspapers should be allowed and which banned, what type of clothing is appropriate and what is not, what music will be allowed and what will not. The sad fact is that clerical policies have generated a great deal of animosity and resentment—an immense disservice to our religious heritage.

The dramatic consequence of the Islamic revolution has been the realization that theocracy is an unacceptable form of government. Iranians, among them an increasing number of highly intellectual and vocal clergymen, are openly debating the merits of secularism—a clear separation of religion from government.

This growing number of clerics and religious intellectuals see no contradiction between modernity and Islam. More importantly, progressive theologians do not see democracy as a direct threat to religion. In fact, the debate in Iran over religion in recent years has been among the most advanced and thought provoking in the entire Muslim world. This advanced thinking is the result of the obvious short-comings of a religiously based government.

It is critically important, however, to clarify that the rejection of theocracy—of an Islamic republic—

does not, in anyway, mean a rejection of Islam. Equally important, separation of religion and state does not only restrict the clergy from interfering in government affairs, but the government from interfering in religion.

Like so many other Muslim countries, Iran faces the dilemma of what to do about calls for Family Law—for example, issues pertaining to divorce procedures and a women's rights to inheritance—which is exclusively based on the Shari'a, the Islamic Law based on the Quran and the Hadith. However, if democracy—representative government—is the order of the day, then these laws must be based on popular will. That being the case, the Shari'a may have an influence over the language of such civil laws, if so wished by the people. The specifics and implementation of these principles should be left to the future constitution, which will need to be drafted and approved by the people of Iran.

Thus I hope to see an end to theocracy, and the separation of religion from government as being in the best interest of Islam and democracy. As outlined above, it would present a unique opportunity for those in the regime to exit politics peacefully.

Seventh, concerning the normalization of international relations, I boldly favor—if certain preconditions are met by the current regime, especially concerning human rights, the media, and the liberation of political prisoners—the restitution of such relations as soon as possible. This will remove unnecessary burdens on the people of Iran. In addition, history clearly demonstrates that totalitarian systems break down faster when there is dialog and openness. The rulers can no longer hide behind walls of isolation, unquestioned and unexamined. Democracy demands that leaders be accountable to their people. This is precisely why many hard-liners in Iran seek to block normalization of diplomatic relations with the West.

Normalization and dialog are not just the concern of governments, but of the international business community as well. As part of this policy, international businesses will naturally be at the forefront of reengagement with Iran. However, such efforts must be conducted with the long-term interests of the

Iranian people in mind: the pursuit of business interest must not be at the expense of human interest.

Eighth, I call strongly for civic responsibility.
Today's problems require the active participation of
our people. In this respect, Iranians need to take much
more responsibility than before. Traditionally, we
have had the tendency to rely overly on powerful leaders to make all the decisions and take all the initia-
tives. By the same token, we as a people have tended
to blame foreign influence and conspiracies for our
ills. In short, "victimization" at the hand of domestic
or foreign forces has been our favorite cultural lament.

How long are we going to blame our misfortunes
on others? When do we take responsibility ourselves?
Clearly, that cannot happen until people are given a
chance to take responsibility. When they are denied
it, they feel frustrated and never develop a civic sense.
The curse of our history is that the public has never
been able to participate in a politically meaningful
way in the system. As a result, we have often felt
either helpless or alienated. That mentality was
prevalent in my father's era and continues today.

Iran cannot forever claim that its backwardness is due to the machinations of others to keep them behind. We need to step up and demand a voice in policymaking, offer ideas, corrections, and accept the consequences. No person or system can afford people happiness or success without personal responsibility.

Today, I sense that the era of conspiracy theory, "victimization," is being replaced by a new era of modern thinking and self-realization. Our people have awakened. They have paid a heavy price to learn the merits of democracy. Our youth are, on a daily basis, pushing the envelope in their quest for self-empowerment. My call for civic duty is embedded in my profound desire to ensure that the old psyche be forever abandoned and replaced by a new sense of national pride in self-determination and rule.

My final point involves the controversial issue of the impact of Western culture on Iranian life. Indeed, this topic has been at the center of a heated debate in our country in recent decades. It is controversial because, despite the many positives the West has to offer, there are negatives as well. Among its

greatest contributions are the principles of democracy, individual liberty, and human rights, which are
compatible with all cultures and civilizations.
However, differing values held by Eastern and
Western cultures continue to fuel a debate about
which aspects to choose and which to leave behind.
Japan is one of the better examples of how Eastern
societies can embrace the best of the West while preserving their own value systems.

Similarly, with a heritage that spans millennia,
Iran is perfectly capable of preserving its cultural
identity and value system while choosing the best of
Western ideals. Interestingly, it is often forgotten
that the best of Western ideals, such as human
rights, pluralism, tolerance, and inclusion of ethnic
and religious minorities, are deeply rooted in our
culture.

Since its emergence, and in order to suppress
demands for political liberalization, the clerical
regime has mislabeled the debate, asking the people
to choose between "West-toxication" and national/
cultural independence.

It is one thing to advocate a rejection of foreign interference in our country's domestic affairs: no patriotic Iranian could argue with that. The issue, however, is not compromising our cultural identity: it is the mechanism by which we can attain real modernization, both politically and economically. We need not become in the least "West-toxicated" in order to succeed. In other words, modernization need not automatically mean Westernization. Clearly, we can build our own Iranian experience with a forward-looking attitude and modern thought, and without alienating the rest of the world in the process.

CHAPTER 2

IRAN AT THE CROSSROADS

he clerical regime of the Islamic republic is now deep in crisis and sliding into decline, and will ultimately reach an impasse. It won't do just to reshuffle a cabinet and reform a few policies. The transformation must be basic and profound: the abandonment of an undemocratic system in favor of a genuine, all-inclusive, and representative government.

As secular forces attempt to gain ground, they face escalating resistance, violence, and spillage of blood. Newspapers are indiscriminately shut down, journalists imprisoned, reformers intimidated, critics silenced, students beaten and tortured, and opposition

35

figures murdered. Daily, we read about riots and
protests across the country. Economic chaos reigns:
while many remain unemployed, those who do have
jobs need to work several of them just to make ends
meet. Unable to secure meaningful employment and
affordable housing, our youth, together with their
parents, are weary of revolutionary slogans and des-
perate for real solutions. In short, political frustration
and economic malaise have cast a dark shadow over
the prospects of recovery, imperiling the future of an
innocent generation.

Failures have also impacted our foreign policy.
Iran's categorization and treatment as a rogue state is
yet another source of national humiliation. The revolution has talked at great length about independence
from foreign influences, but in reality Iran has never
in its modern history been so vulnerable to pressures
from foreign governments as it is today.

Tragically, the most damaging blow to our country's main faith was struck at the hands of a regime
that professed the virtues of an Islamic system, but
failed to realize them by politicizing Islam. Not only

have they made the nation and themselves vulnerable, but they also have ruined whatever respect people might have for politics and religion. Many Iranians today lay the blame on the clergy and on religion itself. The once respected and revered cleric is now the most despised individual in our society. Time and again, I have heard the frustration of the majority of our traditional clerics—those who from the beginning rejected the concept of a theocratic state—who lament the discrediting of our religious values, their loss of credibility, and the sanctity of their establishment. Even some of the revolutionary clerics have voiced similar concerns in their private conversations with me.

The political system as a whole has lost credibility and legitimacy. The ruling clerics are well aware of the crisis: the resentment of the population and the limitations of their own power. The regime faces rising popular pressures. People are fed up, and the Islamic republic can no longer hide behind such excuses as threats from abroad. There is no longer a valid defense to justify our country's inability to regain its once decent and improving standard of living. Iran's dilemma is not just about dress codes; it is about decent employment and housing, higher medical and educational standards, and reduction of the gap between the haves and the have-nots. In short, our story is about basic decency and respect for human life.

President Khatami's surprising election victory in 1997 was a critical turning point in the history of the Islamic republic, representing the first real dramatic break with the system. But the people did not so much vote for him as for a symbol, a split within the establishment, and for a faction seemingly more amenable to basic reform and liberalization. Although Mr. Khatami's achievements during his first term were only token at best, his reelection to office—with a relatively lower margin of public support—was spurred by widespread public fear that any alternative would make life even more miserable.

Previously, in 1993, the people did not actively participate in the election of Khatami's predecessor, Hashemi Rafsanjani. They were cynical about the merits of their involvement in the electoral process. It was assumed that the regime would field its candidate, irrespective of the national sentiment. However, in 1997 and again in 2001, they found the opportunity to take matters into their own hands, the opportunity to send a strong message to the regime, as well as the whole world, that they would no longer be passive, and that they would take a clear step in curtailing the regime's attempt to block reforms. Hence, Khatami's election was in essence a vote of no confidence of the establishment, however limited in choice as being the lesser of the evils.

The 1997 election was a step in the right direction. Khatami was clearly more liberal than earlier leaders, and brought more popular voices into what had been a totally closed system. But his changes were only meant to improve the system of clerical rule cosmetically, not revamp the entire clerical order. Irrespective of his personal qualities, however, Khatami failed to fulfill a single campaign promise in his first four years in office. Not once, not twice, but three times he gained a majority vote during the

presidential, municipal and parliamentary elections.
Yet he lamented constitutional limitations, and
when the students' movement as well as other crises
occurred, he actually sided with the supreme leader
and the ruling establishment at the expense of his
principal constituency. Today, after a fourth round of
elections ushering in Khatami's second term, people
are still waiting for the materialization of his aging
promises, although most of his constituency has
basically lost faith in his abilities to deliver.

The reality is that Mr. Khatami's ultimate goal
has always been to preserve the system, not to change
it. In fact, any other vetted candidate, carefully
screened and filtered through this closed system,
would be charged with the same task.

Alas, this system has proven to be unsalvageable,
and inherently irreformable. It is fatally rigid in its
interpretation of religion and legislation. Decision
making never reaches the level of the people and
their wishes, but instead remains in the clutches of
narrow-minded clerics and pedantic theologians who
articulate the ideology of the ruling establishment to

secure their own positions of dominance and material gain.

Hence, deeply entrenched institutions still oppose
steps towards liberalization and reform. Quasi-
governmental revolutionary foundations like the
"Bonyads" in reality end up representing the private
interests of key regime supporters who have profited
immensely from their privileged position between the
state and the market, stifling free market forces and
entrepreneurship. The court systems, intelligence ser-
vices, and organs of control and repression are all in the
hands of the hard-liners—even the state media. If you
were to take the religious aspect out of the equation,
you would find the rulers in Tehran to be little different from a communist regime in which every move is
fixed to perpetuate and insure its own survival. The
hard-liners have sought to silence any independent
voices anywhere within the media, but their monopoly
of control has been challenged by independent journalists who are waging a courageous struggle in the
name of a free press and honest examination of the
weaknesses of the regime.

Fortunately, the more the regime seeks to reform itself, the more it will be forced to turn to the ranks of competent technocrats. In fact, these technocrats represent the greatest hope for change and progress in the future. But today their hands are tied. Ever-changing regulations coupled with rampant corruption prevent competent civil servants from doing their jobs: meeting goals, finding solutions, and resolving problems.

Today everyone's life is touched at the most basic level by the stifling policies of this regime and by the prospects of democratic reform. More than twenty-two years of theocratic rule and economic chaos have prompted Iranians to demand nothing short of a secular democracy. Indeed, no generation in our history has been as politically aware as today's. They don't have all the answers, but the thinking process is very important. Few, if any, young minds take anything for granted anymore, unlike my generation. By and large, we had material comforts, access to good education, and rising living standards. We were respected worldwide, and enjoyed normal and profitable international relations that helped keep our enemies at bay.

This generation, however, is different. It has suffered enormously and has had to pay dearly through war, political suppression, loss of economic opportunity, and loss of respect from the international community. They are well aware that there is a different world out there, and realize that things need not be the way they are. Today's youth openly question the inadequacies of their government. Dissatisfaction has forced the new generation to think much more politically and to take charge of their fate. They have indeed become more responsible citizens.

This is the greatest asset that any reform movement can hope for when moving towards democratization. In Czechoslovakia, it was the intellectuals under Vaclav Havel who called for change. In Poland, it was the blue-collar unionists under Lech Walesa who led the change. In East Germany, the collapse and abandonment of the security forces, the Stasi, brought down the system. Today, the Iranian environment is ripe for a combination of all such elements to work, all because of the new psyche of the new generation—the emerging "Third Force," with secularism as the cornerstone of its democratic aspirations.

It is important to recognize that people rarely rebel out of misery. It is when things look like they could be improved that people start pushing for change. External reasons can have a course-changing impact as well. The tragic September 11, 2001, terrorist attack on U.S. soil was indeed a rude awakening, but one which has clearly changed the face of the earth in terms of how the world has come to a point of addressing, not just terrorism, but the ultimate reasons that cause such behavior in the first place. Had it not been for a sustained track record of promotion of extremism and hostility, Tehran would have been looked upon in a different light. Today's pressure on regimes such as the clerical one in Iran is yet another element that is forcing the leadership to retreat, thereby giving Iranians one more reason to search for an opportunity to make a move.

Today, the limited degree of liberalization being conceded by Tehran is just such an opening. However, it is clearly not enough. The process of democratization is not a one-way street, and a government cannot simply graciously grant it to its people. Democratization is not given but taken by individuals who demand it. It is a process, and one that mandates the full participation of each citizen. After all, it is the people who must—and eventually will—determine how and what it is that they demand from their government.

CHAPTER 3
OIL, ENERGY, AND THE ECONOMY

he politics of Iran—the nature of the clerical regime, its radicalism, the anachronistic nature of its theocracy, and its internal policies—regularly hit the headlines. What gets overlooked is the immense importance of Iran as an economic power and key player in the development of the economy of the region. Furthermore, with the largest regional population and one of the oldest civilizations of the world, Iran has a vast potential and a great responsibility to maintain peace and stability in the Middle East. Consequently any disturbance and disruption in the proper use of Iran's resources will likely have detrimental consequences for the region and beyond.

At this moment in history, the question preoccupying all Iranians is our country's future. Having one of the youngest populations in the world, how can Iran maximize its natural and human resources in order to meet the aspirations of its 67 million plus people—70 percent of whom are under the age of thirty?

During 1999 and 2000, many Iranians broke the barriers of fear and censorship by openly voicing their anger at the continued lack of freedom and repression, and their disappointment at the failure of the government of President Khatami to fulfill many of its campaign promises. From the point of view of the average citizen, it is the regime's economic failures that bite hardest and create its greatest vulnerability. Unemployment, gross depreciation of the Rial (Iran's currency), inflation, and a stagnant economy are but a few of the regime's mounting problems.

Before the clerics took control of our country, the National Iranian Oil Company produced over 6 mil-

lion barrels of oil per day (mbd). Twenty-two years
later, Iran is hard pressed to produce half that
amount, while the population has practically doubled. Similar to other sectors of the Iranian economy,
the oil and gas industry has been politicized. Hence,
negligence and unabated corruption, coupled with
lack of proper management and foresight, have contributed to a dramatic decline of our mother industry.

Moreover, to keep production at the current
level, according to the government, Iran needs
immediately to put into place an annual long-term
investment package of $3 to $4 billion in order to
maintain existing facilities, plus an additional
annual investment package of $2 to $4 billion to
increase production levels. Many Iranian oil experts
say that the immediate need for investment in the oil
and gas industry is much higher than these official
figures—amounting to a minimum of $100 billion
over the next decade. Since this regime has failed
to demonstrate its ability to utilize its resources
effectively, the only alternative is to attract foreign
technology and investment. But what frustrates this

scenario is the existence of constitutional restrictions and antagonistic laws opposing foreign investment, thereby hampering its flow into our energy sector.

According to Iran's current laws, foreign participation and investment in the exploration and development of both onshore oil fields and offshore projects are carried out under an adverse system called "buy back," which clearly compromises our national interest. These laws have greatly damaged the industry because of their restrictive nature, limiting investment by big and medium size foreign oil companies. By contrast, our neighbor, the Republic of Azerbaijan, since gaining its independence in 1991, and with less than one-tenth of Iran's population—has obtained investment commitments in excess of $50 billion in its energy sector, while Iran has barely managed one-tenth of that amount.

Here it is interesting to note that under the Islamic regime of the past twenty-two years, Iran's total oil revenues of over $300 billion have been more than twice the cumulative oil revenue of the country since the early days of William Knox D'Arcy

(1901), when oil was first discovered in Iran. In addition, the new regime had inherited billions of dollars as international monetary reserves. But due to gross mismanagement, this regime squandered both its inherited reserves and the highest oil revenue in two decades in our national history, leaving the nation with infrastructural and industrial decay.

Further compounding the problem is the use of outdated technology in the development of oil fields. This not only increases production time, but also damages existing reservoirs. Most experts agree that there are at least forty newly discovered onshore oil fields that have not yet been exploited, and exploration with old methods and the lack of modern gas-injection technology has "killed" a great number of oil wells.

Clearly, Iran remains one of the most important oil and gas producers of the twenty-first century. Currently Iran has an estimated 10 percent of the world's oil reserves as well as about 18 percent of the world's gas reserves. But for such a potential to materialize, billions of dollars of investment are required. Our problem is not money. It is the nature

of this theocratic regime, and its pursuit of ineffi-
cient economic and industrial policies, that have
held back the process of modernization. The net
result is that badly needed foreign technology,
know-how, and investment have not found their way
to Iran's key industries.

The hard reality is that Iran's population is pro-
jected to hit the 100 million mark within the first
half of the twenty-first century. The regime has
guaranteed a crisis because it has failed to attract the
type of investments necessary to generate sufficient
revenues to address the most basic needs of its boom-
ing population.

Obviously Iran is going to have to depend on its
energy resources to serve as the backbone of its economy for quite some time to come. The challenge will
be to manage the oil industry as our supplies of oil
gradually come to an end. A high proportion of our
present GNP is tied to the maintenance of the existing and dated oil infrastructure. A visionary, sound,
and responsive government in Iran should plan for the
postpetrodollar era. Here again, myopia has clouded

the clerical regime's foresight. Its fundamental rigidity has disallowed any move towards progress.

However, Iranians should be comforted by the
fact that our country also enjoys extensive reserves of
natural gas, the second largest in the world. Here we
have a great potential for a vast new industry,
thereby extending the window of productivity in our
energy sector.

Additionally, with the emergence of petroleum
industries within the newly independent states bor-
dering the Caspian Sea, as well as Central Asian
states, the strategic role of Iran has been enhanced in
the area of energy transport. Geographically, Iran is
a natural region of energy transit at lower cost than
most other options, such as the Caucasus mountain
ranges or the long distances across Turkey and even
Afghanistan. Iran stands to earn additional income
as a result of significant transit fees. But since the
industrial world depends on these lines, Iran must be
politically stable, and must guarantee security for
such transit. Only Iran can provide access to the
warm waters of the Persian Gulf as the shortest and

most cost-effective way for these Central Asian and
Caspian states to export their energy.

Despite our substantial gas deposits, it is unwise
for any economy to rely exclusively on a single prod-
uct. We need to aim at other areas such as mineral
exploration, especially copper. We should seriously
consider alternative sources of energy for our domestic
consumption. This will enable us to preserve our valu-
able petroleum resources—on the one hand, applying
their usage to more efficient and profitable pharma-
ceutical and petrochemical industries, and, on the
other, reducing the harmful environmental impact of
polluting emissions.

Iran's strategic access to Central Asia and the
Persian Gulf reinforces our geo-economic advantages, which compels us to give priority to the
expansion of our light industries. Products such as
detergents, household appliances, light machinery,
clothing, and textiles have a proven demand in our
neighboring emerging markets. Similar factors
should prompt us to boost our economic expansion
in the area of high technology and electronics. Here

again foreign investment and transfer of technology are essential if we are to excel in this field.

Infrastructure has been neglected far too long. In order to address the basic needs of our society, as well as keep pace with our anticipated growth, we must aggressively pursue the expansion and modernization of our transportation and communication infrastructures. Primary and secondary highway systems and roads, bridges, and high-speed railway systems are among the most important areas needing immediate attention.

In recent years, decaying radar systems, outdated navigational ground facilities, and the slow process of phasing out old planes have caused great concern over the safety of air travel in Iran. The once proud Iranian civil aviation industry needs to be quickly revamped. Failure to address this issue will not only place our own citizens at risk, but it will also exclude Iran as a viable strategic hub for international aviation and commerce.

In general, Iran still remains a very attractive field for foreign investment. But we need much more infrastructure as well as well-trained cadres in order to satisfy the requirement of our growing population. In addition to the aforementioned needs in the areas of communications and transportation, additional housing and various new educational and medical facilities must be given high priority.

At this point we lag significantly behind international standards in the area of technological skills. With the drastic decline in the quality of education in our universities and training centers, and a lack of sufficient and well-trained educators and instructors, Iranians can only feel frustrated. Our young generation, which promises to be the most important factor to fulfill our various development and modernization goals, bears the brunt of this lack. Annually, about 1.5 million anxious high school students compete for about 85,000 places in Iranian universities. That's a ratio of almost 18 to 1. At the time of this writing, there is only one job for every twenty-three graduates. In other words, over 90 percent of the best minds remain unemployed or will not find a job befitting their academic achievement and expertise.

Developing our own technological skills will also help free us from the traditional trap of foreign technical dependency. Much of the money spent on foreign experts should go to develop our own educational base. Iran, similar to many developing countries around the globe, would not want to waste national income on supporting high foreign salaries. The generation of a domestic, highly skilled training force will help us steer clear from such dependency down the road.

What Iran lacks is not a hard working labor or white-collar force; it is the state of our economy that has made it very difficult for people to find decent jobs. With dismal salaries and insurmountable problems associated with a depreciating currency, on the one hand, and dramatic increase in prices for goods or housing, on the other, our population has been impoverished—nearly 50 percent living under the poverty line. The rate of unemployment is simply unacceptable by any standard. In short, while our national income, both in real as well as nominal terms, has fallen substantially below what it used to be before the revolution, our population has since doubled.

The bottom line is that the current political situation in Iran is at the core of the problem. Realistic policies, as well as significant and tangible changes in our national and economic priorities, have yet to materialize. Despite numerous promises made by the current government, nothing has really changed. Vows of reform and liberalization have proved but empty slogans. While the major preoccupation of the ruling clerics has been to shuffle faces in an attempt to dupe the outside world into seeing "moderation" and "normalization," Iranians themselves have lost faith in this regime's ability to make a breakthrough.

As demonstrated in the demands articulated by the frustrated youth of our country, the need for political reform and liberalization is the cornerstone of our people's aspirations. Any improvement in our socio-economic situation can only be brought about through democratic change—a change that can only occur in a postclerical and posttheocratic era. Here again, outside the regime's core group, theologians see no conflict between religion and modernity. However, they openly concur that theocratic rule is in direct conflict with democracy, and inimical to religion and the clergy as well. Once more, the conclusion points to separation of religion and government as the key pre-requisite, and the only remedy to our national illness.

Despite the current state of affairs in Iran, I remain highly optimistic about the economic and political future of our country. We already have a ded-icated work force, as well as sufficient resources. What we need is a major change in domestic politics, as well as in our international relations. A government truly of the people can and will bring us back into the world—it will empower our gifted and young citi-zenry to apply themselves fully to building our future prosperity.

CHAPTER 4
FOREIGN POLICY

or nearly two centuries, external influence and, at times, intervention has played a central role in the way Iran has viewed and positioned its foreign policy. Our struggles to preserve and protect our sovereignty and territorial integrity have molded the Iranian psyche, while the country pursued its relationships with other countries.

Iranians are proud of having successfully resisted multiple attempts by covetous foreign powers to colonize or control our country. Our nation is vividly aware of its history, which has included invasions, wars, and frequent manipulations of our domestic

61

affairs by external forces. To this day, our minds are heavily influenced by such experiences.

Today, Iranians expect a foreign policy that stands firmly for Iranian rights and national interests. Our people also recognize, however, the realities of an interdependent world, which requires of its community of nations civility and cooperation as opposed to radicalism and hostility. Hopefully we are now at a stage in Iranian history where we can achieve some balance in viewing the international order—cherishing our independence and self-determination while seeking to work constructively with the world community.

As Iran enters the new millennium, it finds itself in a region filled with potential flashpoints. To our north, the Caspian basin offers our region newly found opportunities with significant new oil and gas reserves. This clearly translates to long-term regional economic exchanges and cooperation, with Iran as a central and strategic link between Central Asia, the Caspian basin, and the Near East.

Yet the same region is rich with hotspots that may unleash disruptions. We are currently witnessing a

state of unresolved conflict and friction between
Armenia and Azerbaijan, with which we are geographically, historically, and culturally linked.
Throughout history, Iranian-Azaris and Iranian-
Armenians peacefully coexisted within our border. In
view of this cultural link, a credible, democratic, and
stable Iran would have a natural role as an honest bro-
ker in resolving this and other similar crises. In the
post-Soviet era, it would be mutually beneficial to resurrect the multifaceted bonds that have existed
between Iran and its northern neighbors for centuries.

To our northwest, Turkey offers an important
bridge to Europe. Our relationship has historically
been based on mutual respect and a thriving trade.
Turkey's experience with secularism has long been an
interesting regional model providing intellectual
debate. In view of current circumstances, it is
unquestionably a core issue at the forefront of most
political arguments challenging the current clerical
regime. In recent years, by contrast, elements of mis-
trust have been sown by Tehran's desire to promote
internal unrest and ideological exports. Apart from

neighborliness, the fact that nearly a quarter of Iran's population is composed of Azaris and other Turkish-speaking citizens makes it even more imperative for Iran to reclaim the warm state of relations our two nations have historically enjoyed.

To our west, Iraq, with whom we have experienced long-term border conflicts, remains an important cornerstone for regional security. Iran's devastating eight-year war with Iraq came at a great cost. It will be a long time before Iranians can put behind them the cold statistics of more than half a million dead, more than a million crippled and maimed, and several million displaced. Beyond the human toll, it will take decades and cost billions of dollars to rebuild destroyed cities, villages, homes, schools, hospitals, industries, and historic landmarks. The greatest tragedy, however, is that the Iran-Iraq catastrophe was a conflict of personalities and individual ambitions, driven by unadulterated egotism. The Iraqi people have paid as dearly as their Iranian counterparts. Our futures are inevitably tied and must be based on a shared commitment to

mutual respect and regional stability. The democratization of both nations will undoubtedly contribute
to a stable and reliable relationship.

To our east, Afghanistan and Pakistan are two
countries with which we have historically enjoyed
friendly relationships. However, at the time of this
writing, Afghanistan is experiencing a tragic turmoil under the harsh and radical policies of the
Taliban, further exacerbated by their association
with Osama Bin Laden and his organization's recent
terrorist attack against America. The Afghans, similar to their Iranian brethren, are witnessing the suppression of their deeply rooted cultural values, as
well as their aspirations for modernity. One of the
most outrageous and tragic consequences of the
Taliban regime has been the brutal repression of
women in Afghanistan—a heartbreaking issue well
understood by their Iranian counterparts who are
still experiencing the agonies associated with their
treatment as second-class citizens.

Pakistan's nuclear arms program undoubtedly
has a direct impact upon Iran and the immediate

region. Our neighbor's long-term stability and security is the only guarantee of the containment of the proliferation issue. Since its birth, Pakistan has enjoyed a relationship with Iran based on mutual respect and common values. As a friendly neighbor, Iran can be an important partner in promoting regional and socioeconomic cooperation, which would contribute to Pakistan's long-term stability.

Highlights of recent decades underscore the global strategic value of the Persian Gulf. It not only serves as the energy lifeline to the industrial world, but it also is the umbilical cord nurturing the very prosperity of its surrounding states. Despite recent cosmetic warming of relations, ever since its inception, the clerical regime of Tehran has targeted its southern neighbors with its radical ideological exports. If Iran is to contribute towards a peaceful and stable region, our relations with our Arab neighbors must be based on genuine friendship, cooperation, and mutual trust.

Beyond our immediate region, Iran is as interdependent with the world community as any other country. The xenophobia imbedded in the mentality of a handful of radical theocrats should not be confused with the thinking of our open-minded citizens. As Iranians, we are not unique in having a strong sense of nationalism, pride, and desire to maintain our cultural identity. But given our deep desire for modernity and advancement, we must embrace global interaction, which brings with it knowledge, technology, and overall progress.

Iran's current foreign policy, which has been set in the background of militant anti-Americanism, has a clear record of pursuing a mix of "revolutionary fervor" with anti-Western hostility. This policy has resulted from a need to establish a legitimacy, which is far from secure at home. However, as is evident in the recent cosmetic niceties emanating from certain elements of the regime, Iran can no longer afford to isolate itself from the very same quarters it must rely upon for future financial investments and technological know-how. Hence, contrary to earlier lines pursued by its propaganda machine, the Islamic regime has tried to counterbalance its continuing hostility towards the U.S. by offering major dubious and opaque concessions, clearly in conflict with Iran's national interest, to other Western powers as well as countries like Russia, China, and North Korea.

In our look towards the future, we must focus on two fundamental issues: our partnership with the global community, and our need and desire for self-determination and cultural preservation. Contrary to the dogma underlying this regime's foreign policy, global partnership, self-determination, and cultural preservation are not incompatible.

CHAPTER 5
THE IRANIAN DIASPORA

tragic consequence of the Iranian revolution of 1979 is that we have today over three million Iranian expatriates scattered all around the globe. With the United States and Canada playing host to more than a million, another third live in Europe, while the rest are scattered from Latin America to the Far East and Oceania. The departure of hundreds of thousands of skilled professionals from Iran has been a stunning loss. Writers, poets, singers, physicians, scientists, engineers, officers, lawyers, diplomats, academics, and many other experts had, reluctantly, to bid farewell to their motherland for fear of persecution and even death. Sadly, even after more than twenty-two years, this exodus continues. Last year alone, according to official government records, 220,000 of Iran's best minds left the country, most probably never to return. The loss of such human talent, which would have otherwise been in the service of our country, is simply beyond calculation.

Empty promises, coupled with continued repression at home, have left people with an obvious sense of neglect, frustration, and outrage at the overall living and human conditions in Iran. Apart from a limited group of cronies with a vested interest in keeping this regime in power, the clerical regime has failed to bring the rest of the nation together in order to apply its multitude of talents. The regime has also failed to persuade the expatriate community—in which are some of our brightest minds—to return to our homeland and participate in the advancement of our country.

After two decades of stressful readjustment, by and large most Iranian expatriates have managed to establish themselves within their respective host countries, often very successfully. But few of them can ever fully forget that they live far from their mother country, deprived of their identity. To be unable to live freely in one's homeland, and to enjoy its landscapes, scents, tastes, dialects, and wonderful traditions, is a heart-wrenching tragedy for all of us, especially those who have had to endure this painful separation for over two decades.

The first task of a future democratic government in Iran would be to attend to the immediate needs and priorities of the people, such as jobs, housing, health, and education. But that government must also plan for the repatriation of many members of the diaspora, as well as implement various programs that would engage the expatriate community in contributing in a variety of ways to their home country's progress. The Iranian diaspora is a great hidden asset for the future of our homeland. Many of its members are by now well established in their new homes and societies and integrated into the political, economic, and social life of their adopted countries. With a new generation of Iranians coming of age outside of their land of origin, they have for the better part prospered in all walks of life and assumed leadership roles in various sectors—starting businesses, running for public office, administering hospitals, banks, research facilities, and scientific entities at the highest levels, becoming law enforcement officers and civil servants, and joining the ranks of highly respected scientists, researchers, and artists.

Only a sound and reliable political system will lure such gifted patriots to return and enhance the future of Iran. A visionary government committed to our future generations will have to awaken nationalistic fervor and inspire our diaspora to commit their resources to the service of their homeland. This human, intellectual, and financial capital must be mobilized in order to complement the existing resources within our borders. Together, these dedicated Iranians will have an opportunity to maximize their potential and impact our future.

Our countrymen in the homeland, of course, represent the vast majority of our national human assets. They are directly involved in daily political life inside Iran, yet they also face the powerful restrictions, even dangers, from the rigid political order imposed by the clerical regime. Iranians abroad, on the other hand, have full political freedom to speak and act, but by definition are absent from daily political life in Iran. They are excluded from direct participation in its political order and therefore have limited influence. This reality calls for complementing roles—a division of tasks—between the two groups, in which each has something unique to offer the other.

In all this, it is indeed tragic to witness Iran's loss of the constructive contribution of at least two generations of expatriates that could have helped propel our country into the twenty-first century. There is no doubt in my mind that if Iran had not undergone a revolution but instead had evolved peacefully, by now it could have been economically on a par with many of the so-called "Asian Tiger" countries. Unfortunately, a regime with a medieval mentality sidetracked the efforts of the previous generations, forcing the people to cope with repression, poverty, and unemployment at home, as well as exile and asylum abroad.

After the traumatic experience of the revolution and its consequences, we cannot undo overnight all the changes that have taken place, nor should we. It would be naive, even arrogant, to think that those who have been living abroad for two decades or more, or who have grown up abroad, can just go back as if nothing had ever happened. And those that stayed in Iran have their own concerns and anxieties. We need to be sensitive to the fact that there might be some potential resentment on the part of those who stayed behind towards those returning. However, our compatriots at home should look at the positive aspects of the repatriation of new talent and information, as well as some degree of Iranian wealth from overseas that will move back into the country. All this should be welcomed as an additional asset for Iran.

Conversely, I would expect my compatriots abroad not to forget that it is those who did not leave who have had to bear the most severe hardships. They are the ones who have been struggling within the system for over two decades and who have pushed to bring about as much progress as possible in spite of the hard-line clerics.

There may be particular resentment towards some of those who chose to leave on purely economic grounds. But their lives outside the country have not necessarily been rosy either. They have often undergone various kinds of malaise, depression, suffering, loneliness, discrimination, and displacement, and now look forward to returning. People who had served in the high echelons of their former society have had to take much humbler positions abroad and lose the recognition and prestige they once had. For many others, religious minorities for example, departure was almost a necessity because of a real threat to life and property. Others faced nearly certain persecution on a political or ideological basis.

In the end, the desire of various Iranians to return to the homeland demonstrates some basic love and commitment to their country. I hope we can all deal with this sensitive question that involves feelings that are understandable on both sides. Indeed, in view of our overriding national agenda, we must strive to overcome such emotional hurdles in the shortest time possible. Both groups of people have unique skills and, in the end, depend on each other.

Countries that learn to attract and harness their intelligentsia from the very start have the best chance of developing functioning democracies and successful societies. The terrible thing about dictatorship is that it shuts out constructive criticism, the voices of those who see better ways of doing things. These dictatorial regimes pay the price for decades by being deprived of the best ideas their intelligentsia can provide. With our talented diaspora on the outside, and the cadre of professionals on the inside, and of course the unswerving dedication of every single Iranian, we have more than enough to trigger a dynamic explosion of intellectual and economic energy as well as greatly improve our chances of establishing a successful and thriving democracy.

CHAPTER 6

CONSTITUTIONAL
MONARCHY

or over twenty-five centuries of re-
corded history, the institution of monarchy has been one of the main pillars
of the Iranian nation. However, the
passage of time has brought about new concepts and
ideas, including those about governance. I see the
potential role of the monarchy today as significantly
different from what it has ever been before in the history of our country.

As an important factor contributing to historical
continuity, the monarchy has, throughout the millennia, provided the Persian Empire with stability and
preserved, for the most part, our nation's territorial

77

integrity. But a twenty-first-century monarchy must
be inherently different from those of the past and can
only be perpetuated by remaining strictly constitutional and operating within the framework of a truly
democratic society. In other words, the monarch
would be a symbol for the nation, but in fact not
responsible in any shape or form for the affairs of
government.

Having said that, I firmly believe that self-
determination and popular sovereignty continue to be
the overwhelming and long-standing desire of our
people, and a vital priority upon which our whole
future depends. While many argue that the immediate problems in Iran are economic and social, the roots
of these ills lie in the political nature of the current
regime. As we witnessed in the final days of the former
Soviet Union, the final salvation came as a result of a
change in the system as a whole and not just some
liberalization of its policies. In other words, the problem was not necessarily due to the leadership of a
Stalin, Brezhnev, or Gorbachev; the problem was
ultimately systemic, and the system itself had to go.

Likewise, the problem in Iran has nothing to do with the personalities of the current leaders. Regardless of what one might think of Mr. Khatami and the authenticity of his discourse, he is just as much crippled by his own system as Gorbachev was at the end. The Islamic republic as a system is bound to collapse as it reaches an unavoidable impasse. One cannot reform what is inherently immutable. Therefore, Iran's only salvation lies in our ability to promote freedom, and we must grant top priority, in the context of our national identity and cultural preferences, to the installation and implementation of a completely democratic system as rapidly and smoothly as possible.

There are currently two possible models of democratic governments in the world—a constitutional monarchy, and a democratic republic. As heir to the Iranian throne, I am regularly asked about my views on the role of a monarchy in a modern Iran and its compatibility with democracy. I will reiterate some key points here:

First, a constitutional monarchy is as compatible with democratic order as a republican form of government. Today we can find good examples of each model in prosperous, free, and independent states such as Spain, Sweden, France, Germany, Japan, Norway, the United States, Canada, and several others.

Second, under a constitutional monarchy, the head of government is clearly the elected prime minister, not the monarch. The first misconception of most proponents of a republican system for Iran is their assumption that the monarch would both reign and govern. A second misconception is that because the monarch inherits the position and is not subject to an electoral process, the people have no choice in leadership, and therefore democracy is compromised. Again, to counter such a claim, I would argue that it is the prime minister—comparable to an elected president in a republican system—who is in charge of policies and decision making, and not the monarch, who is a symbol of unity and stability for the nation, but not a figure responsible for the governing process.

The best way for a monarch to serve the country is to be the guarantor of the constitutional process

and to protect the constitution itself. This would
certainly be the case in Iran. He or she must be
immune to vulnerability and criticism by remaining
detached from the day-to-day running of government, which would be the responsibility of an
elected prime minister.

The monarch must be above all political factions
and be neutral, unbiased and impartial vis-à-vis all
ideological, ethnic, religious, or other social and political groups. Only then could the monarch be a true
unifier of the country, the cement bonding a multi-
ethnic nation and heterogeneous society. With such
ultimate legitimacy, long-term stability is further
guaranteed. It is also important to note that the special grooming and training of the heir to the throne
since birth brings him or her a unique qualification for
this honorable task. Beyond intellectual faculties, the
heir to the throne has the privileged opportunity to
develop personal appreciations for different countries
and their cultures as well as cultivating relationships
with a variety of political, cultural, and academic
personalities worldwide. Such an experience can only

benefit the nation without the monarch having to be directly involved in government.

The key resemblance between a constitutional monarchy and a democratic republic is the fact that the person who is in charge of government is indeed elected by the people. For example, in Great Britain, the prime minister is elected in a national election. Such is the case in Canada, in Holland or in Belgium. In the United States, Germany or France, a president is elected. However, in a republican system, we find some variations. Some countries have a nongoverning president as head of state with an elected prime minister as head of government, such as India or Israel. Some countries have only the president as commander in chief and head of the executive, such as in the United States or South Korea. In some republics, we see both a president and a prime minister in charge of government—sometimes from a different political party—such as in France.

Notwithstanding such variables, in all of these countries the person in charge is an elected official. In the case of the monarchic systems—whether it be, say, Queen Elizabeth, King Juan Carlos, King Carl Gustav, or Queen Beatrix—none of them is held accountable for the affairs of their respective governments. As heads of state, they represent their nations, while no one questions the democratic nature of the governments of those countries. So when I speak of a constitutional monarchy as an alternative or option for Iran, I would point to these examples as probable models.

Third, even though as the heir to the throne I represent the institution, I do not consider my immediate role to be that of an advocate of monarchy itself. Rather, I see my current role to be that of an advocate of the needed democratic and peaceful process of change in Iran today. If the people of Iran are to choose a constitutional monarchy or a republic by means of a national referendum (a decision that would determine my own future), we must first set the stage for such a decision process to become a reality. It is in this context that I find, at this crucial time, any debate between the merits of one system versus the other to be premature and divisive, and something that could only delay the progress of a much needed change in Iran.

I would never want to be a cause of polarity and division. Quite the contrary, my role is to be a catalyst and a provider of unity. Therefore, I stress the fact that all of this is not about me, but the cause of freedom for Iran and Iranians. Furthermore, while Iranians have different persuasions, and therefore view my role from different perspectives—monarchists as their king, republicans as a political figure—I have never allowed such a diversity of opinion to cloud the overall concept of our collective need for unity by promoting democracy in Iran as a national priority and as our common denominator.

Fourth, out of the more than 67 million people of Iran, I find myself in a unique position as the only person with the historical burden of representing the institution, albeit today as a potential option. So long as the Iranian people, in a genuine referendum, have not decided the fate of this institution, I have the duty to represent it to the best of my ability. For those who would argue that such a referendum did take place in

1979, I would suggest that that process was certainly not free and fair by any stretch of the imagination. In addition, it should be pointed out that nearly three-quarters of today's population had no voice in that decision. Having said that, the true voice and opinion of Iranians today, who are certainly unable to express their real aspirations under the current regime, should be given the opportunity either to confirm their acceptance of the current system, or determine the regime and political structure of their choice in the future. Again, it is on these grounds that I believe that, well before we discuss and debate the merits of a republic or a monarchy, we must first have an open political environment.

Furthermore, what matters at this time is the content of the future regime. The fundamental issue for Iranians is to attain self-determination through the democratic system, thus guaranteeing the representation of candidates from all political parties in the electoral process. Regardless of the ultimate form of regime, the future governments of Iran will be formed as a result of a genuine democratic process.

Fifth, I personally believe in the advantages of a constitutional monarchy over a republic for Iran at this time in our history. If I didn't, I would not have accepted my duties as heir to the throne twenty-one years ago. Part of my reasoning has a lot to do with the nature of Iran itself as well as our Iranian culture and mentality. For example, if we were to look at the United States in comparison to Iran, we could ask ourselves this question: Would an American living in Buffalo feel closer in terms of cultural identity— not to mention tribal, ethnic or religious in the case of Iran—with a Canadian living in Toronto, or with a fellow American living in El Paso? I suppose the answer would be the person in El Paso. On the other hand, if you asked a Sunni Baluchi living in the southeastern part of Iran whether he felt culturally closer to a Shi'a Azerbaijani living in northwestern Iran close to Turkey or Iraq, or to a Pakistani Baluchi living a few miles across the border, the answer would be the latter.

So, while national unity in America is not directly related to the role of an individual in the system, in Iran the monarchic institution has in fact been the key element in preserving national unity. Taking into account Iran's rich cultural and ethnic diversity, as well as migrating tribes and nomads, one could understand how Iranians have valued their symbol of unity throughout the centuries. The same weight and importance is given to the merits of this institution in Iran today, perhaps even more than before the revolution.

The possible disintegration of Iran is a legitimate concern, and not an insignificant threat in the long run, should the current trend of affairs remain unaltered. This is one area where a symbol of unity could make the difference. On another plane, given the fragile nature of a newly established democracy, the very same symbol of unity could maintain stability and unity during the period of institutionalization of various components of the overall system, as well as the growing civil society. In recent years, the best example was King Juan Carlos of Spain's crucial role in lending stability to the post-Franco era, when a young Spanish democracy was seriously threatened by a potential right-wing military coup against the socialist government. This is further testimony to the fact that, for a constitutional monarch, it makes no difference which political persuasion is represented in government.

As far as I am concerned, it will be just the same to me if our future prime minister is a representative of a conservative party or a socialist one. It goes without saying that any Iranian who qualifies for the job should have an opportunity to participate in government, regardless of his or her religion, ethnic background, or other personal or social orientations. This is the future I envisage for Iran, and if called upon by my compatriots to serve as their monarch, I would vehemently defend these principles in accordance with my duties to preserve our people's rights and protections against any kind of discrimination as articulated in our future constitution.

Having said that, Iranians may still opt for a republic. They may have reached a point where they no longer feel that they need a monarch as a symbol to preserve our national unity, among other reasons.

An intimate moment between father and son: watching sports on television.

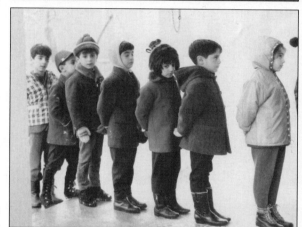

Standing in line before entering a classroom.

Taking notes in class.

A typical family dinner.

Praying at the tomb of "Imam Reza" in Mashad.

Reading news reports in Panama.

Getting ready for a training flight in an F-5 in Tehran.

A winter outing in Farah Abad, Tehran, on my horse "Palang."

In my soccer uniform during my pilot training days at Reese Air Force Base.

Being enthusiastically hugged by supporters.

Addressing compatriots in a packed
sports arena in Los Angeles.

A daring candlelight vigil in Tehran following the sinister September 11, 2001,
terrorist attack on the United States.

Taking calls from supporters during a live interview at KRSI studios in Los Angeles.

With my brother, Ali Reza,
at our mother's home.

My father: I took this photo in Cuernavaca, Mexico.

Leila, my late sister, whose untimely death has deeply affected me.

With my daughters, Iman and Noor.

With my wife, Yasmine, in early 1990s.

Iran's supreme leader, Ayatollah Ali Khamenei.

Young students protesting against the regime's attempts to quash freedom of speech and freedom of the press.

Supreme leader
Ali Khamenei and President
Mohammad Khatami,
below a poster of
Ayatollah Khomeini.

A student protester throwing rocks at riot police in Tehran.

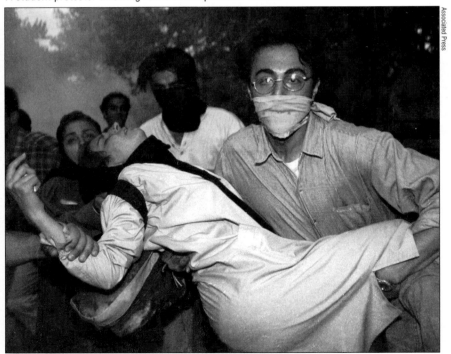

A student carries a fellow wounded protester in front of Tehran University.

This issue is not limited to Iran. As a matter of fact, recently two countries, Sweden and Australia, have exercised such an option in referendums on whether they should keep their monarchical system or switch to a republican system, albeit for different reasons. Evidently, the majority in both countries decided that the status quo was fine.

The bottom line is that Iranians should have a choice—one that ought to be made in a free and untainted environment. Like all people around the world, Iranians have the inalienable right to decide their own future. In a sense, this will bring closure to a dark period in Iran's history and simultaneously open the nation to a new and bright era. I would consider my mission accomplished the day Iranians go to the polls to make their decision. Frankly, I am not at this time concerned about what will happen to me. If called upon to assume my royal duties, it would be the greatest honor bestowed on any individual. If not, in terms of my personal convictions, I see it as my civic duty to discharge my responsibilities to my homeland and state, albeit as a simple citizen.

Sixth, it is important that Iranians look beyond
me as the messenger and understand the message
itself. Fortunately, many of my compatriots today
have risen to the occasion and appreciate the need, at
this critical juncture in our evolving history, to promote unity among groups and organizations of different political and ideological persuasions, and a
consensus at the national level to commit all their
resources to the restoration of self-determination.

In the past twenty-one years, I have relentlessly
played my part by advocating the need for cooperation and unity among all those who agree with this
principle. In order to facilitate the process, I have
worked closely with many of my compatriots on
strengthening and expanding this arena, both
among opposition groups in exile, as well as various
leaders and organizations at home. As access to Iran
becomes easier, we are hard pressed to establish more
and more contacts within Iran—particularly with
the new generation and the intelligentsia.

We should, as a nation, have faith in the process
and trust each other's sincere commitment to our
common goal. So long as we all respect the rules of

the game—the democratic process—we should also respect the outcome. It is in this light that I would like to set an example and be the first to respect the choice made by the majority of Iranians. Because I firmly believe in the foresight and political wisdom of my fellow compatriots in making the best choice in an environment free of persecution, intimidation, and despotism, I invite all to have faith in this democratic process. If we believe that the future constitution will guarantee each person's rights under the law of the land—regardless of whether one belongs to the majority or minority—we should have no fear of the outcome.

Finally, at this crucial time in our country's history, it is important for my compatriots to understand fully this major and perhaps most important point: I consider my role to be that of encouraging a transitional, nonviolent process of change while advocating no specific outcome—except the restoration of self-determination. I invite all Iranians to participate in this process, and for all of us to set the appropriate political environment and stage to determine our political future.

CHAPTER 7

NONVIOLENCE AND CIVIL DISOBEDIENCE

ne of my fundamental beliefs with regard to our national struggle for freedom in Iran has been nonviolent action and civil disobedience against the clerical rulers. I am fully aware, however, that many of my compatriots may seriously doubt the likelihood of political change in Iran without violent confrontation and bloodshed, particularly in view of the regime's record of ruthless repression, assassination, and tyranny.

Nevertheless, as a student of history, I base my convictions on the power of the people and their ability to do what it takes through sheer will,

determination, organization, and planning. Most
recently, we have witnessed a dramatic unfolding of
events leading to the deposition of a feisty Slobodan
Milosevic in Yugoslavia. Even more dramatic was
the way the old Soviet Empire simply crumbled
without bloodshed, a violent coup, or even assassinations. Indonesia, South Africa, and Chile are other
examples where the mighty could not hide behind
brute force and repression against nonviolent actions
and the resistance of the masses.

As far as Iranians are concerned, we need not
look far to find counterexamples of such phenomena:
i.e., Iran's own 1979 political upheaval and the violence that the Islamic regime has since inflicted on
Iranians. Two decades later, our nation is being
crushed by the iron grip of one of the most brutal
regimes it has ever seen. While the world is in search
of twenty-first-century solutions for peaceful coexis-
tence and socioeconomic progress, Iran's clerical
regime is obsessed by its struggle to command and
control the will and desires of a nation.

History has provided us with two fundamental
lessons: The first is that political change as a conse-

quence of violence—be it a classic military coup, an assassination, or civil war—more often than not results in the replacement of an undesirable political situation with one even worse. Nonviolent action for change is based on the fundamental principle that the means will determine and influence the end. In this respect, if our national objective is to attain freedom, democracy, and long-term political and social stability, the means to achieve such a goal must be as worthy as the goal itself.

The second lesson has been learned in recent decades, during which the world has witnessed dramatic political change in numerous countries ruled by unpopular and undemocratic regimes. In nearly all cases, such changes were brought about as a result of important and effective nonviolent movements, which included well-organized and well-publicized civil disobedience campaigns. In my view, the important lesson is not merely that unpopular regimes will inevitably fall, but that no matter how brutal or ironclad, they will eventually succumb to popular will. Moreover, we have learned that when the popular will is expressed through nonviolent resistance and civil disobedience, it generally results in the establishment of a democratic political system.

Examples of Nonviolent Campaigns

Organized mass struggle and nonviolence have a long history and involve the refusal to counter the violence of a repressive system with similar means or methods. A dramatic and often emulated technique of nonviolent resistance and defiance was Gandhi's bold, yet peaceful, campaign for India's independence from the British Empire. There are, however, many other examples, concerning both domestic problems and foreign interventions.

American revolutionaries staged tax and tea boycotts against the British. Two centuries later, the U.S. civil rights movement called for nonviolent resistance and actions such as sit-ins, freedom rides, voter registration drives, jail-ins, and the like. The 1960s witnessed opponents of the Vietnam War employing tactics such as draft card burnings, mass demonstrations, and tax resistance. Since the mid-seventies, nonviolent civil disobedience has taken place at dozens of nuclear weapons research installations, storage areas, missile silos, and corporate and government offices, in opposition to the arms race. The anti-apartheid movement of the eighties staged daily protests in front of the South African Embassy in Washington, D.C., joined often by members of the U.S. Congress, as well as religious leaders, celebrities, and students.

By no means is civil disobedience and nonviolent action a modern phenomenon. As early as 494 B.C., plebeians in Rome decided not to kill the consuls who refused to answer their grievances but instead withdrew from the city to a hill, which became known as the "Sacred Mount." After a few days, significant improvements to their lives were granted.

The people of the Netherlands nonviolently resisted Spanish rule in the 1560s, and Hungarians resisted Austrian domination in the 1850s.

Jewish lives were saved in Denmark and Norway when those nations used nonviolent methods during the Second World War to stop the "Nazification" of their school systems.

During the 1960s and 1970s, the Salvadoran people's version of nonviolence included occupations and sit-ins at universities, government offices, and factories by student groups and labor unions.

Berlin witnessed, in 1920, the defeat by nonviolent action of a rightist coup d'état against a legitimate German government. A similar situation occurred in the Ruhr in 1923. In 1986 the people of the Philippines peacefully overthrew Ferdinand Marcos. In the spring of 1989, the world was stunned when hundreds of thousands of Chinese demonstrated and fasted for freedom of speech and democratic reforms. Tiananmen Square was filled with thousands of Chinese students holding signs reading "We Shall Overcome."

And today, in Iran, the students and youth are leading a national charge for secular democracy through a multitude of nonviolent methods of civil disobedience. Sit-ins, silent marches, street protests, newsletter/pamphleteering, and calls for boycotts by student leaders and organizations have inspired similar acts of protest, strikes, and in some cases even riots by discontented workers, farmers, and parents, as well as members of the oil and gas industry.

Only a few years ago, Iranians dared not speak out against the ruling clerics, but today they are openly voicing their anger and boldly defying the regime in cities, towns, and villages throughout Iran.

This is a lucid example of how nonviolent action and pressure exerted by the people can result in reform. Iranians need to keep pressing ahead until they can attain a secular government, a civil society, and a real democracy based on the will of the people.

What Does Nonviolent Action and Civil Disobedience Mean?

My conviction that nonviolent action is an effective method for bringing political change in Iran is based on the fact that it ultimately yields comprehensive and permanent results. Although some may assume that "nonviolence" implies passivity, it is in reality a potent and active form of resistance. That is because nonviolent civil disobedience involves people—en masse—taking active roles, making choices, and being collectively committed to a clear course of action. Often, such movements are based on particular principles. In the case of Iran, it is based on the principles of secularism, liberal democracy, and a civil society.

Desperation and a lack of self-confidence may indeed engender hate and a wish for revenge in people's hearts and minds. I regularly find these emotions and hear cries for help from my suffering compatriots. Because of a false sense of helplessness, they often demand nothing short of a swift, forceful, and unforgiving "iron fist" to destroy the enemy overnight, thus clearing the path to freedom. They would easily condone violence for the sake of salvation.

But any change based on political violence only results in partial rectification of the original problem. Especially, since acts of political violence are often directed at the command of a limited number of people, such acts are rarely inclusive and do not facilitate a broad participation by the masses, thereby failing to translate into a necessary precondition for achieving a stable and permanent democracy.

My philosophy is not based on seeing our national struggle as a "rescue mission" alone, but as one that will plant the seeds of permanent political stability and the institutionalization of democratic principles and a civil society.

The strength of a nonviolent movement based on civil disobedience is that it is based on mass support. It encompasses all sectors of society, and it is all-inclusive in nature. Ultimately, it can even provide those on the other side with a way to submit peacefully to the will of the people.

It is imperative that Iranians today look beyond revenge or calls for blind violence, and discard myths that suggest we are not yet ready to take collective charge of our destiny.

The Road Ahead

In our national crusade for personal and political freedom, we must remain committed to our ideals and avoid acting like, and thereby becoming like, our oppressors.

I must insist on this point more than ever. If history has taught us anything, it is that repeating mistakes dooms us to relive the same tragic consequences. I do not believe in choosing a path that will give us only a temporary respite. I adhere to the school of thought that aims to eradicate a basic problem permanently, no matter the cost and the duration of the process. In other words, it is not enough just to ease the pain; we must identify and permanently cure the disease.

Only through a profound evolution in our collective psyche, cultural awareness, and intellect can we as a nation attain the sort of modernity and political liberty suited to the twenty-first century and beyond. We must embrace our cherished principles of nationalism, patriotism, independence, sovereignty, and cultural identity, but also graduate to the next level—rebuilding our society by taking charge of our own destiny. No mysterious hand, no miracle, no savior can hand this to us on a silver platter.

What we must never lose sight of—and what will ultimately decide our national fate—is our commitment to fashion our destiny by implementing our ideals and by putting these thoughts into action. We must work for it and earn it—together!

CHAPTER 8

THE INEVITABLE
IMPLOSION

he Islamic republic of Iran, as a political system, has reached an impasse.
More than twenty-two years after its
inception, it has shown neither the
ability nor willingness to implement meaningful economic reforms or political liberalization. Although it
has been given the benefit of the doubt by a more-
than-patient society, this clerical regime simply cannot continue to sustain itself in power and faces
inevitable implosion. Rifts and divisions among different factions of the regime have become even more
apparent in recent years, and the internal disintegration will only escalate. An incompetent and corrupt

theocracy is not what the people intended to attain
with the revolution, and all eyes are now turned
towards the opportunity to attain a better political
future. But the way in which the regime will collapse
is of critical importance, because it will profoundly
affect the nature of any future government.

Prerequisites for Change

First, the internal situation in Iran has to be ripe for
change. True, a harsh and determined authoritarian
regime is not easily removed—as we have witnessed
in the case of certain military dictatorships or totalitarian communist regimes. But the situation in Iran
has evolved, and the prospects for positive change are
greater. The fragmentation within the ruling establishment has increased and widened the gap between
rival factions.

Ever since the Ayatollah Khomeini's death, a
clerical clique has ruled Iran. But even that clique
has been smart enough to recognize that it does not
have the people's backing for most of its policies.
They too lived through the revolution twenty-two

years ago and are well aware of the danger of serious public disorder—even anarchy—if the heavy public pressure for change is consistently ignored or crushed. As a result, we now have a society ripe for fundamental change.

Unlike the outside world that still believes moderation within the Islamic regime is possible, Iranians have come to the conclusion that the ruling theocracy is inherently incapable of liberalization. Even if the ruling clergy were to recognize the need for fundamental change, the biggest stumbling block remains the constitution of the Islamic republic itself. For instance, while everyone was hoping that Khatami would indeed be able to implement his campaign promises—a position that earned him an overwhelming vote, especially among youth and women—he could not in fact act upon it, simply because he would have had to violate the letter of the law. It is important to realize that the constitution ultimately is based on divine law and that the supreme leader, or "Vali-e-Faqih," in this case Ayatollah Khamenei, has full discretion to interpret the law as he sees fit, and

can override or veto any legislation. In short, the leg-
islative body, and for that matter the head of the executive, represents nothing more than a mockery of
what they claim to be a democratic system.

The people's frustrations and desires, especially
among the intellectual elite and youth, are boiling
over into fierce public debate in the press, even though
the regime has tried to silence as many writers and
newspapers as it could. Even some of the initial members of the reform movement, who earlier advocated
some legal reforms within the context of the current
constitution, are now questioning the feasibility of any
such reform. The basic conclusion now reached by
many, including the students and some of Khatami's
supporters, is that only a secular government can effectively implement true reform and establish a genuine
democratic system. As I noted earlier, everything rides
on the successful separation of religion from the state.

Some members of the ruling clergy admit that
they will be swept away if the regime fails to demonstrate a serious commitment to change, even though
they still believe in some modified religious govern-

ment. Meanwhile, the silenced traditional clergy has maintained from the beginning that direct rule by the clerics will in fact damage the clerical establishment, and with it religion itself. Such a forecast is vividly demonstrated in Iran today, after twenty-two years of theocratic rule. I therefore believe that, for the first time in over two decades, we have a promising setting for bringing about major change. With care and national determination, the secular movement will culminate in a genuine democracy beyond the current regime.

As another precondition, the movement requires organizations both inside and outside the country that will reinforce each other in order to facilitate the process of change. Change is not going to come about simply because people want it, or because the clerics decide to extricate or vote themselves out of power. The clerics will never voluntarily give up power and grant democracy. Only under popular demand and unswerving pressure can they be forced to relinquish power and yield to the people. Therefore, the role of the democratic opposition, both at home and abroad, is essentially to serve as a conduit for popular feelings and aspirations.

But having organizations in the opposition is not enough in itself. The various opposition elements, especially those abroad, have to work together more effectively. Those at home, who have been mostly organizing themselves as underground groups, face the important task of joining hands at some point in the name of a collective effort. Only such an organized "coalition" of forces at the national scale will allow Iranians to go on the offensive and direct the process of change, and practically dictate terms to the regime, on their way to securing a new political future.

The primary task for political activists abroad, in my opinion, is generally twofold: first, the rallying of support from the Iranian expatriate community— both in terms of intellectual and financial contributions—for our compatriots at home and especially for the flag bearers of our struggle, namely, our students and various groups within our intelligentsia; second, to direct towards the international community a well-orchestrated information campaign aimed at raising public awareness and sensitivity to the realities of Iran.

As we witnessed in the case of South Africa or Yugoslavia, overwhelming public demand was capable of pressuring democratic governments, in particular, to adjust their foreign policies by steering away from business-as-usual approaches and towards support of a democratic process of change. Likewise, Iranians would greatly benefit from knowing that, after more than two decades of practical neglect, this time the world was truly rallying to their support. The people of Iran would receive a clear signal indicating that those governments will not favor the continued rule of the current establishment in Iran for the sake of preserving certain economic interests. Rather, true to their stated principles and in defense of human rights and freedom, they would no longer tolerate any actions by the current regime in violation of such principles. Iranians demand nothing more and nothing less than what was done in the case of other oppressed nations.

Meanwhile, it is just as crucial to remember the importance of unity among the various opposition

groups for the sake of our national cause. Any digres-
sion into premature ideological debates or insistence
upon personal political agendas will irreparably harm
the liberalization movement. As mentioned before, the
opportunity to advocate one's ideas and policies will
certainly arise, as long as we remain focused on bringing about a favorable climate and appropriate circumstances for a genuine referendum and free elections.

Despite the importance of such international
attitudes, I am still concerned that differing percep-
tions compounded by short-term interests between
Washington and Europe have made it difficult for
the West to arrive at a consensus on how to handle
the situation in Iran. For other power blocs such as
Russia and China, their policies towards the region
have changed little since the end of the Cold War,
fostering similar reactions as in the past towards
Europe and especially the United States.

Propelled by the pursuit of commercial gains and
the infamous "oil factor," many states have unfortunately shown a callous disregard for the welfare of our
people and the state of human rights in Iran. Despite

several successive administrations—both under a Republican and Democratic White House—it appears that the U.S. government has not been able to move beyond a self-imposed foreign policy of "dual containment" and economic sanctions.

Although some diplomatic overtures were made in the waning days of the Clinton administration, the futile quest for "moderates" within the regime as a whole has thus far forced a deadlock on any major shift in policy towards an eventual normalization of relations with Tehran. Even worse would be the pursuit of a different, but still detrimental, attitude of opting for an "appeasement" policy.

Economic Sanctions

The quest for political change by Iran's population and the prospect of new U.S. policies under the George W. Bush administration make this the most propitious moment for U.S.-Iranian relations since the advent of the clerical regime.

The genuine struggle taking shape in Iran today pits the forces of state despotism against an emerging

popular movement that rejects Islamic fundamentalism, repudiates the "supreme rule" of Ayatollah Ali
Khamenei, and views the newly "reelected" Khatami
as an already spent political force.

The young emerging third force fully recognizes
that Khatami's brand of theocracy and extreme militancy are inseparable, just as theocracy and democracy are incompatible. These youths already know
that the Western leaders' belief that Khatami will
prove to be a genuine reformer in his second term is
a vain hope. More importantly, they know the
Western policies that reward Khatami in anticipation
of such reforms fly in the face of twenty-two years of
clerical rule in Iran, and of dictatorship in general.

Under the guise of religious piety, Khatami and
Iran's other theocrats have fostered political repression, economic decay, and moral corruption. They
have turned Iran into a pariah state while denying
the Iranian people their basic rights, and have driven
nearly half of the population into poverty—through
"elections" in which the regime vets and chooses
candidates. It resulted in a supreme rule devoid of

every tenet of modern justice and civil governance, in state-sponsored terrorism, in the pursuit of dual-use technologies and weapons of mass destruction, and in the overall mismanagement of the economy due to nepotism, graft, and the plundering of our natural resources.

The U.S. administration and Congress are right to condemn these pillars of the clerical regime's rule. Now, however, the time is right to spread the focus of Western policy to Iran's internal development. This is in part because change will almost inevitably come from within Iran. Washington and its allies should offer political and moral support to the Iranian people. They should foster democratic development through indirect assistance to the emerging movement against the regime. Through the new opportunities presented by the Internet and other technologies, they should promote the dissemination of unbiased information to give Iran's young people hope and a tangible means to turn their democratic aspirations into reality.

At the same time, any viable policy by the United States and its allies to promote a democratic

Iran must include a responsible sanctions policy vis-à-vis the regime. In my view, efforts to lift sanctions unconditionally are misguided. Any relaxation should be linked to meaningful improvements in Iran's human rights record, such as the release of political prisoners or lifting the bans on a free press and political parties.

If such improvements occur, however, the United States may want to consider, inter alia, extending export credits for agricultural and medical sales to nongovernmental entities in Iran, permitting the sale of personal computers and software to the Iranian people, and permitting the sale of civil aircraft and maintenance parts so that Iranians can avoid the horrors of flying unreliable, Soviet-built aircraft.

Among the strongest agitators for reduced sanctions are the U.S. energy companies. Unfortunately, Iran's oil supplies constitute not only an economic boon, but also a political lifeline for the current regime. In this area, it is imperative that sanctions not be relaxed and foreign firms not be allowed to do business in any way that strengthens the regime and thereby facilitates its repression of the Iranian people.

In a democratic Iran, where the rule of law and financial transparency will prevail, Western companies will be able to explore, develop, and transport Iran's vast oil and natural gas reserves fairly and competitively, and not on the backs of ordinary Iranians.

The rewards of U.S. leadership on this issue are clear. It is vital that Iran, the most populous and arguably most strategically significant country in the Middle East, become democratic. A free Iran will find common ground with the West on political issues in and beyond the region, play a constructive role in international organizations, offer a moderating role in the Arab-Israeli peace process, furnish a reliable corridor for the flow of Caspian oil and gas resources to international markets, and bring stability to the Persian Gulf and the Strait of Hormuz—a strategic route for the transport of two-thirds of the world's energy supplies.

The Opposition Abroad

It would be crucial at this stage for the foreign-based opposition to facilitate the means, and provide various channels, of communications for interested governments and international political, as well as nonpolitical, entities to work in tandem with domestic opposition organizations. Additionally, the role of the international media, as exemplified in liberalization processes around the globe, is crucial. For this reason, Iranians at home would be best served by an all-out effort by the vocal expatriate community to divulge as much accurate and detailed information as possible about what is actually occurring daily in Iran. This could very well force Tehran to permit the fledgling democratization process to continue. Events are moving in the right direction now. Iranians outside the country are catching their second wind, greatly encouraged by the activities of their compatriots on the home front.

It has been a source of concern that, while our young generation at home has been undergoing a political awakening and a shift in mentality as a result of the hard realities of the current regime, some individuals and groups in our exile community have had difficulty in leaving the past behind. They instead pursue political ideologies that are out of touch. Whether or not there is a change of perspective among these exile groups and individuals, events in Iran will not wait for them to catch up.

I sincerely believe that if we are to assist our youth in their quest for freedom, the last thing we should do is to encumber them with irrelevant issues from the past. I would also vigorously argue that no one, starting with myself, should think that the people of Iran should be patronized or dictated a preconceived outcome. We should trust our compatriots' ability to make responsible decisions for their own future.

Far too often I have heard arguments favoring strong leadership. I have faced a lot of criticism by a variety of people, often blaming the lack of progress on my personal reluctance to play such an aggressive role. I find it odd that the same people who once blamed my father for exceeding the boundaries of his authority and accused him of being a dictator, ended up blaming him for not having acted strongly enough to prevent the revolution from happening. Ironically, people of a similar mentality today are asking me to assume the very same role, forgetting that this created the political crisis in Iran before the revolution.

I am not certain whether such individuals have learned the lessons of history, but I know that I have. No matter what is said or will be said, I will not betray my conscience and the best interests of my country by falling into the same trap again. I do not deny that charismatic leadership has its merits and that someone like me could play a big part in assisting in the introduction and institutionalization of secularism, democracy, and civil society. It is my firm belief, however, that my greatest task as a leader would be above all to share my experiences and humbly provide my fellow compatriots with all the knowledge and skills that I can offer—in essence, teach fishing, rather than be the person who delivers fish to their doors.

Having said that, I do not shy away from my duties and responsibilities. I am simply suggesting that in today's world the leadership of just one individual is no longer feasible; that leadership must be distributed among different layers, both vertically and horizontally. It is with this premise that I have approached our struggle from day one. It will be in this same spirit and belief that I will continue to play my part in this collective process. I have clearly expressed my opinions to many leaders within our community, and I hope that the rest of our society will understand the merits of this approach over other traditional, but unrealistic and impractical, approaches.

The Collapse of the Regime:
Four Possible Scenarios

With a new attitude among those of us who are committed to the cause of freedom, we should be prepared for a variety of possible reactions that this regime might have at the prospect of its demise. I suggest four basic possibilities:

The first scenario envisages a nonviolent evolutionary process by which the regime gradually evolves out of its authoritarian character, yielding increasing democratic concessions in response to public demand. Eventually, a parliament votes to hold a nationwide referendum on reforming and abolishing the current constitution, and along with it clerical rule and the Islamic republic. If once there were arguments favoring reform of the current constitution, such an approach is falling out of favor with each passing day. The chief reason is that, even if the position of the supreme leader were transformed into a publicly elected office, as opposed to the complicated web that masks the despotic nature of it, the very idea of an infallible leader, especially an elected one, seems quite incongruous. If he is not truly infallible, then why should he have the final word on all issues? And if fallible, then what is the point of the position? Can the correctness of Islamic law be debated, and parts of the Shari'a be defeated in parliament? This is damaging both to the democratic process as well as to Islam itself.

Meanwhile, by maintaining a peaceful and gradual approach to the process, the transition between the old order and the new becomes seamless and there is no violence or breakdown of law and order. The most crucial element here is the readiness and coordinated effort of all prodemocracy groups and organizations to work together and assume the delicate and vital leadership during the transition process. This would be the most sensitive period in our historic evolution; any failure to manage this phase properly will result in another catastrophe, perhaps even graver than what happened in 1979.

The advantages of this scenario, of course, lie precisely in its peaceful nature. It avoids a moment of breakdown or collapse of authority and possible anarchy in the interim, and it would most likely enjoy broad international support and encouragement, even offers of financial assistance in the process. It is the ideal scenario in many respects. However, one should not be so naive as to think that our counterparts in Tehran would be as magnanimous. The regime's track record of terrorism and assassination of political opponents both at home and abroad makes it hard to imagine that the clerics will agree to go that easily. After all, few dictatorial regimes ever willingly give up the old order—of which they are the chief beneficiaries. It will be particularly difficult for the supreme leader to give up a position that is symbolic of everything the Islamic republic stands for—rule by clerics in the name of Islam as they see it, not to mention material gains for its mostly corrupt leadership. Thus, in practical terms, it is unrealistic to expect that Iran can move out of its Islamic republic predicament quite so painlessly.

In the second scenario, the transition to a democratic regime takes place, but not so smoothly. Here the clerics realize that the ship is sinking but are unable to abandon it. A frustrated and angry population realizes that the process of liberalization is neither fast nor thorough enough to satisfy urgent requirements, and that the regime is incapable of making a decisive break with clerical rule. As opposition forces mount in parliament, pressing the regime ever harder, the regime tries to play for time. Khatami, or any future would-be reformist, even if he supported the forces of reform all the way, is blocked by the hardliners and a deadlock emerges. As a result, the media defy all censorship controls and open a broad front against the regime—albeit by resorting to underground tactics and "night pamphlets." International public opinion calls for the regime to acknowledge widespread opposition and to step down peacefully. Defections from the regime become widespread and public clashes with security forces become commonplace. Large portions of the regime's supporters lose heart and abandon it, leaving only a hard-core resistance in place. The public takes matters into its own hands and stages demonstrations, protests, and strikes, calling for a referendum on the future of the regime and demanding that the supreme leader step down. In the end the clerics are forced to yield to popular opinion and allow the people to determine a successor regime through unrestricted parliamentary elections.

This scenario is a promising one, but also contains numerous risks since it involves the collapse of power and the serious problem of an interval of confrontation and transition between a past and a future government. The possibility of a general descent into anarchy in the absence of legitimately constituted authority is serious.

In the third scenario, the regime resists to the bitter end, using its militias or even specially trained and previously hidden intervention units, with complete disregard for mass casualties. The immediate outcome would be a militaristic and totalitarian regime that would cancel all previous experiments with liberalization and democracy. Reformers would be crushed and jailed, even assassinated. Any pretense of Islamic legitimacy would vanish. The international community would obviously condemn the regime, and it would sink into deeper isolation. Change would be delayed indefinitely, and only a long-term armed struggle could eliminate the regime. Although the regime could hold on by sheer force for some time, deteriorating circumstances would lead to another revolutionary situation. Unfortunately, this very negative scenario cannot be excluded.

However much the international community condemned such a course of events, we must be realistic in the sense that we could not seriously rely on physical intervention from the outside to halt or change the internal situation. If a coalition of international forces were unwilling to intervene even to help bring down other tyrannical regimes by direct interference, such an intervention in Iran would be virtually inconceivable, absent a war scenario. A real danger, however, is that a potential foe might exploit Iran's internal turmoil, as we saw happen shortly after the revolution by Iraq. Such an intervention would almost certainly spark a foreign response. At a minimum, one could hope for strong international rhetorical support—official governmental condemnations and statements, United Nations resolutions, diplomatic pressures—all on behalf of the Iranian people in the event of a violent and irrational crackdown. But none of these actions will deter the regime in the short term. Iran could be in for a prolonged period of dictatorial rule, yet again.

A fourth scenario envisages the regime deteriorating into internal chaos of warring factions including Mafiosi-type groups, all struggling for control over the regime, access to power, and influence. Their respective militias, engaged in armed combat, would begin to move towards serious civil war. Opportunistic, and not necessarily democratic, forces might find backers in the military, so the whole country could be at war until one faction succeeds in asserting its dominance. Such a scenario would be disastrous for the population and possibly even the infrastructure, if fighting raged in the main cities of Iran, a la Beirut of the late twentieth century.

Worst of all would be the emergence of separatist movements, some representatives of which have already started the rhetoric of secession and independence, which could result in a Yugoslavia-like disintegration of Iran. The whole political map of the region would have to be reassessed. Furthermore, such new alignments or newly created sovereignties might threaten former Iran's immediate neighbors. As often seen on the European continent, our part of the world has had its share of bad blood as well.

As terrible and dramatic as this scenario would be, it seems less likely since the regime's interest in staying in power has so far prevented any serious internal conflict, and the military has stayed out of politics. But it is very unlikely that democratic forces could emerge victorious in a scenario of civil conflict and violence. Under such circumstances, victory usually goes to the most powerful, most ruthless, and often minor, yet opportunistic, force, to the detriment of the silent majority still committed to democracy. Iran, or what would be left of it, would be stuck under another long bout of authoritarian rule, not necessarily better and perhaps worse than what we have now.

The Likely Course of Events

Clearly, the first scenario—a peaceful dismantling of the clerical regime by legal process in the parliament—is the most desirable way to go. I would encourage every Iranian to sincerely follow it, and I appeal to the representatives of the current regime to take this opportunity to abandon power peacefully. But it is probably naive to expect the regime to go so quietly, yielding its control of state institutions and declaring the end of the Islamic republic.

The second scenario is much more likely, whereby the regime drags its feet in the face of demands for reform, and an angry population takes matters into its own hands. There will be a nationwide call for the regime to yield power to a self-appointed transitional commission or temporary coalition government to hold a referendum on the future, as well as draft or revise the appropriate constitution. I think it is likely that a public confrontation will take place, but one that, hopefully, will avoid a descent into serious civil conflict or anarchy.

For this reason, my strategy for the future is based on contingency planning for either of these first two scenarios, and is designed to keep the situation from deteriorating into the general chaos of the third and fourth scenarios.

The heart of my strategy towards the current regime is to provide the ruling clerics with an opportunity for a peaceful exit from the political arena, and to ensure that the situation remains within the bounds of the first or second scenarios. But of course, when you talk about an exit strategy, you have to assume that there actually is an intention to exit on their part. Recently, I have received specific information as to the willingness of certain prominent members of the regime, as well as highly ranked members of its militia—some of whom have personally met with me—to declare their willingness to cooperate and help in the process.

Some people may question the sincerity of their claims. Yet, I can relate to the actual feelings and beliefs of a revolutionary guard, for instance, who is about my own age and who has today realized the consequences of what he at some point believed to be a sacred duty. They too have witnessed the injustice of their mentors, and are no longer willing to turn their guns towards their innocent brethren.

I am convinced that the current leadership knows it has largely lost the religious credentials it once had. All they have to do is look at the election results to see the people's willingness to vote for anything that moves them away from clerical rule and towards democracy, liberalization, and openness. Not all the leadership may yet agree that clerical rule as a concept is over, but the idea is sinking in ever more rapidly at all levels.

A Call to the Ruling Clerics

At this point, I openly call for the ruling clerics to permit a bona fide national referendum and to be prepared to step down peacefully if the nation votes against the continuation of the Islamic republic. The clerics in leadership, more than anyone else, have to be concerned for their own safety and welfare in the face of what could be angry mobs bent on revenge. Only their own security forces are able to protect them at this point, but they are no doubt wondering who will protect them as the system collapses.

I cannot predict what would happen under a new republican system. If I have a leadership capacity in the future, however, and insofar as it is within my prerogatives as king, I am prepared to offer the clerics sanctuary and protection from likely spasms of "revolutionary justice" from aggrieved citizens, much like what took place in the early years of the Islamic republic. The ruling clerics most likely realize that there is no group, political party, or national leader in a position to protect them from the wrath of the people in the long run. Only the monarchy, for historical reasons, has the legitimacy and moral strength to call for calm, restraint, and reconciliation among rival political groups. The monarchy has never opposed religion or antagonized the clergy over the past centuries. In a legitimate secular state, this could continue in the future.

Indeed, I know from my own contacts with the clergy that many of them are actually counting on this contingency in the future to avoid just such revenge. Having said that, I cannot and will not preempt a legal process of judicial inquiries related to victims' claims against gross injustice, corruption, and criminal action by the former authorities. By the same token, it is evident that the accused would have legal recourse in terms of having a right to a fair trial with full legal representation in a proper court of law. A rule of law that is founded on the principles of the UN's Universal Declaration of Human Rights is the first step in reinforcing our democratic goal, while cynicism would be democracy's worst enemy and therefore should not be allowed to develop.

The key to success in this scenario is the position taken by the regime's own forces of repression, especially the militia (Basij), the Revolutionary Guards (Pasdaran), and other special units. These coercive forces, more than any other element in the regime, have to be concerned about their own future. It is true that most of them have courageously and honorably defended the nation in war and suffered great casualties. But unfortunately, some of them were swayed by greed and corruption, and have maintained certain privileges by trampling the rights of their own brethren. If the system fails, they have reason to be concerned about what could happen to them. They, like some of the clergy, want insurance from a lynch mob. Many of them have given up hope and fully realize that this system can no longer deliver what it once promised, or could even protect them in the end. So they especially look to some ultimate leadership, outside of this system, which can offer such protection. This point is perhaps one of the most significant issues directly related to the process of a genuine and long lasting national reconciliation, which, in my opinion, is the foundation stone for our future prosperity, stability, and a successful democratic order.

Indeed, such offers of protection are very important to the ruling clergy and its militia, and would likely give them real hope that even they could be players during the transition and not necessarily its victims. It is foreseeable that the isolated ruling clerics at the top of the pyramid would try to convince their militia not to trust the democratic opposition, and to believe that anybody who would enter the scene will be absolutely and categorically dedicated to their utter destruction. This would be their final hope of keeping these elements from defecting. That is why I believe an exit strategy should be offered—one that invites all those former supporters who are now disenchanted within the regime to break with it in favor of our national movement for freedom and democracy.

What, then, is the obligation of these people if they hope to survive the collapse of the regime? From this moment, they must refuse to use force against the people—as some have recently demonstrated—

against students activists, our women, our youth, or any citizen seeking freedom and justice. The security forces need to be seen as being on the side of the people. Once the regime perceives the defection of their own security forces, they will understand the futility of further resistance to popular will. Indeed, many leaders are already buying time at the present, opting to become observers of the scene rather than being actively engaged in the system. More than anything else, such widespread anxiety and disaffection within the coercive forces of the regime indicate how fragile and susceptible it has become.

Some elements may still believe that they must stay with the regime to the bitter end, for three main reasons: because they do not see any way out of the present collapse of the system; because they still believe the regime can hold its ground; or because they have deep personal and material interests in holding onto power. Once again I would remind them that real power is ultimately in the hands of the citizenry; they can perhaps buy some time, but ultimately time will run out.

I am encouraged to see that the majority of the most menacing elements that could have been a main obstacle to our struggle are today demonstrating their willingness to join our ranks and fight beside us. The rest of the regime's apparatus will have little incentive to hold on to the very end. I think we may be astonished at how fast the regime implodes as these realities become clear. The more intense the opposition becomes, the more defections will occur.

Three Sectors of Iranian Society with Decisive Political Influence

Who will be the key actors in the collapse of the clerical regime? Principally, three social sectors will play decisive roles:

The first consists of the politically active members of the intelligentsia: students, academicians, journalists, writers, intellectuals, professionals, doctors, white-collar technocrats, and so on. These groups take a keen interest in politics, are generally opposed to the clerical regime, and are involved in political activity where permitted. They will constitute the front line in challenging the regime and demanding that the system be opened.

Second, we have a traditional sector in Iranian society that has historically exerted political influence by being the principal backer of the frontline political activists. This group is centered in the economic sector: businessmen, guilds, and workers who can be mobilized into action in times of political tension and confrontation. But if we are to develop a coordination process among various antiregime elements, we must think in advance about who does what and when during a time of crisis, and about the sequence of actions under different contingencies. The bazaar (Iran's traditional economic sector) and the traditional clergy are key players, but we probably can't expect them to take the initiative against the regime before the intelligentsia does and before the sharp decline of the regime becomes quite evident. Provincial elements and tribes are also part of this ensemble. This sector is in a position to cause disruptions through strikes and general civil disobedience. Ultimately they could seriously cripple or entirely shut down the economy—the classic warning signs and forms of opposition we have witnessed in Iran.

Finally we have an unknown quantity in other key social segments, such as some of the clerics within the regime, as well as the military forces and the Revolutionary Guards. The latter are linked at the moment with the regime, but their actual political state of mind has yet to be publicly manifested. The militia plays a key role in particular because it can refuse to cooperate with the regime against the people, such as crushing student activists who demand democratic rights. My aim is to reduce to a minimum the number of elements that would fight against us to the bitter end.

But how do we mobilize the intelligentsia and the technocracy within the present system? How can they press the regime, not only to exercise the rights that they currently might have, but also to go beyond that? We need to ensure that they will be able to express themselves in ways that help form a true civil society. Efforts from entities such as the Writers' Guild or other professional groups—medical doctors, scientists, university professors and schoolteachers, technicians, and other experts—need to reach a broad audience. A tremendous pool of talent also lies within the diaspora, including some of the best minds the world has seen. Together with their compatriots at home, they should raise their voices to remind the government that the present circumstances are utterly unacceptable and that we must push for decisive change. We can therefore discourage hard-liners from any thought of blocking popular sentiments. Foreign-based radio and television, which have broadcast live programs to Iran, have provided Iranians with an effective dialogue while putting further pressure on the regime which can no longer monopolize the airwaves.

The regime needs to be under constant pressure from the people who will push for greater liberalization wherever there is an opening. Even an event like a major soccer match can provide unexpected results. When Iran won a game during the 1998 World Cup, crowds poured into the streets and women threw off headscarves in a way that the regime could not control. Around the time of this writing, serious clashes erupted in a stadium following a match between two of the most popular soccer teams in Tehran. The crowd chanted boldly antagonistic slogans against the regime and called for a national referendum. Once again, the regime resorted to use of violent force in order to curb the spontaneous eruption of protest. Recently, in the aftermath of the terrorist attack on the U.S. on September 11, 2001, Iranians gathered in large numbers and held candlelight vigils while chanting slogans in support of and sympathy for America. As expected, the regime cracked down on these demonstrators. These examples have served, among other things, a great purpose: that of separating the people of Iran, in the eyes of the world, from their unpopular regime.

Constant pressure from all levels of civil society is essential. In its absence, the process could be dragged out forever, with the government only offering small concessions here and there in order to stay in power. Success will come only if we can lend help to these liberal elements and activists. We can support them by breaking the barriers of isolation through the establishment of direct communication and dialog with the support of various focus groups. Unlike the past two decades, today many Iranians are able to communicate with the external world and even travel abroad. They get to see plainly the reality of the world with their own eyes, thus gaining even more political sophistication and encouragement. They are further inspired to tell their stories abroad. Likewise, many Iranians who have lived abroad for many years have a wealth of information and suggestions to convey to their compatriots at home—something they could better achieve by traveling to Iran.

Meanwhile, the current leadership has called for cultural exchange. But it should not be limited to senior policy advisors or to senior professors from one or another American or Iranian university, but should rather be open to all activist elements of society. Furthermore, those in the outside world must realize that the regime has yet to display a willingness to

conduct a civilized dialog with its own people—
never mind one with another civilization.

Overall, by bringing momentum and direction
to the process of change, we could expect for the
world community not to remain indifferent, but to
react positively and encourage our people in their
quest. Such encouragement proved to be instrumental for nations such as South Africa, Poland,
Nicaragua, the Philippines, Indonesia, and others at
a critical juncture in their struggles to eliminate
unwanted regimes or unpopular governments.

But ultimately, Iranians have to be in a position
to make their own decisions, and that will most
likely happen naturally. Meanwhile, the outside
world needs to be sensitive to this developing
process within Iran. The people will welcome international involvement and support, but not at the
expense of losing their independence and cultural
identity. Actually, similar situations exist all over the
world today. But the international community
remains a critical factor: Just how will it react?
Will it stay aloof, just looking after its own narrow

interests, or will it take a broader interest in the problem?

Support for the people is the core issue. Graphic images and other tangible evidence are pivotal elements at this stage. The photograph of the single Chinese student standing in front of a tank in Tienanmen Square had great impact on world policy towards the government in Beijing. Rioting and violence in Indonesia also affected international thinking on the future of the Suharto regime. Sustained street demonstrations on the streets of Belgrade finally forced Milosevic out of power—world indignation rendered his stubborn resistance futile. Nonetheless, as much as such support would inspire our people, the reality is that our country's isolation discourages the presence of a large number of international observers, especially the world media, who could help us tell our true story abroad. Most of the world community does not really know what the people of Iran actually want. Thus far, it has been difficult to collect evidence inside the country that could positively influence public opinion abroad. This is bound to change, especially in the era of the

Internet, provided that world observers, and the media in particular, look more towards these outlets of public expressions rather than to limiting their input to what the propaganda machine of the regime feeds them.

For my part, a key role that I can and will play in all this is to maintain and broaden contact with diverse elements of the population, opposition groups inside and outside the country, and coordinate some advance thinking. But I am not under any illusion that I could control all these forces. They have to be persuaded of the validity of this approach by their own convictions and for the sake of the country's future. However, I will continue to provide an element of hope and vision, based on my faith in my compatriots' abilities and convictions, at a time when so many people are uncertain of what the future holds, not knowing how Iran will emerge from this political dead end.

Domestic Operations

I am regularly in touch with leaders inside Iran, both through my own direct contacts and channels, and through external opposition organizations. Many different types of organizations are involved. Many of these contacts and related organizational works are covert, particularly because there are operatives inside Iran in sensitive roles. They form networks extending into the regime to provide inside information which are ready to act, when the right moment comes, to assist in paralyzing the regime. These activities have to remain secret, since their revelation would obviously hurt those who are cooperating with me and who are committed to future action. Their operations are coordinated via underground channels that, for the greater part, have been preserved. Knowledge of these operatives is on a "need to know" basis, linked to various chains of command.

It is critically important that these activists refrain from prematurely revealing their existence, because actions taken against the regime while it is still in control would have only symbolic value and would be quickly crushed. I have always insisted on the preservation of life and refuse to consent to any operation solely for the sake of demonstration, at the expense of the premature and unjustified death of valiant patriots. It is vital that these groups remain committed to move only when the time is ripe and the regime is beginning to lose control.

At this time, one of the biggest remaining hurdles is the need for serious and widespread material and logistical support by our community for all these networks and organizations at home and abroad. Every single Iranian, regardless of personal wealth, can and must, within the limits of their means, assist in this process and partake in this struggle. Now that the opportunity for meaningful change has finally arisen, it is our duty to get involved and demonstrate strong commitment to the liberation of our homeland.

CONCLUSION

hile I do not expect the regime to simply lie down and allow alternative democratic forces to take over, I also believe that many of its members are sensible enough to grasp the reality that surrounds them. Many have already been arrested or interrogated under suspicion of being in touch with me or other opposition groups. Yet many people from inside Iran are contacting me openly, with no concern for any reprisal, thus making it increasingly hard for the regime to make this a political offense in itself.

People, particularly the youth, are responding to me not necessarily because of my name, but because

they are thirsty for new ideas, new visions, and a
future that offers personal freedoms, liberalization,
democratization, unity, and positive change. Nor is it
in the interest of the regime to push events towards a
bloodbath in which there will be no winners.

Certainly the regime will grow paranoid over dis-
cussions like this about its inevitable demise, but the
more transparent the process is, the quicker the regime
itself will perceive the direction of events and the need
to conform with powerful national sentiments.

Many elements are already present to bring
about change. We have the basic resources needed to
spark it and, most importantly, a majority of citizens
willing to commit themselves at the moment of
truth. For my part, paramount to all other concerns,
I guarantee my best efforts and hard work and, above
all, a sincere commitment to the ideas and principles
that I have set forth in this book.

Furthermore, I continue to work with existing
political organizations, both at home and abroad.
And regarding the world community, I bring our
national message of peace and deep desire for liberty

and democracy to the attention of concerned governments, public or private entities, as well as academic
institutions and the media, with the hope that they
in turn adopt the Iranian cause as they have done in
the case of other reform-minded nations.

Iran is now entering one of the most dynamic
phases of its internal development. Winds of change
are blowing through the cities and villages of my
homeland. We all feel it. More than ever before, we
are ready to assert our overwhelming desire to establish a lasting democratic government for the first
time in our history.

ACKNOWLEDGMENTS

ver the years, there have been so many people who have inspired, educated, stimulated, challenged, helped, loved, and supported me. It has been a long journey, often lonely and at times painful, but I have never lost sight of where I want this journey to end.

Apart from my relatives and close friends, there are hundreds of people who have, in different ways, affected my life and my thoughts. I cannot list them all here, and even if I could, there are many whose identity I cannot divulge under current circumstances. One day—I hope soon—I will be able to publicly thank them.

Most importantly, my biggest source of inspiration, and what has given me heart and will to give my life in pursuit of this cause, are the valiant youth of Iran. Their passion and courage in facing adversity and repression will forever be etched in history. I bow my head to them. I have faith that they will conquer evil, restore our stolen pride and dignity, resurrect our national identity, and revive Iran's glorious name and civilization. I hope I will be there to witness it.

May God protect Iran.